Large Classes

by Rob Nolasco and Lois Arthur

Essential Language Teaching Series

General Editor: Monica Vincent

MODERN ENGLISH
PUBLICATIONS

First published 1988
Reprinted 1989, 1990, 1991 (twice), 1993

Published by MACMILLAN PUBLISHERS LTD
London and Basingstoke

Printed in Hong Kong

British Library Cataloguing in Publication Date

Nolasco, Rob
    Large classes. – (Essential language teaching series)
    1.English language – Study and teaching – Foreign speakers
    I.Title   II.Arthur, Lois   III.Series
    428.2′4′07   PE1128.A2

ISBN 0 – 333 – 43672 – 5

Contents

Acknowledgements

The author and publishers would like to thank the following for permission to reproduce material:

Addison-Wesley Ltd for extracts from *New Horizons in English* by Mellgren and Walker

Cambridge University Press for extracts from *Keep Talking* by F Klippel, *Communicative Methodology in Language Teaching* by C Brumfit and *Reading Choices* by David Jolly

Heinemann Educational Books for an extract from *Teaching Practice Handbook* by Gower and Walters

Longman for an extract from *Practice and Progress* by L G Alexander

Oxford University Press for extracts from *Resource Books for Teachers – Conversation* by Nolasco and Arthur, *Speaking: Elementary* by Rob Nolasco, *Streamline English Departures* by Bernard Hartley and Peter Viney, and *Project English* by Tom Hutchinson

John Wiley & Sons for an extract from *Explorations in Classroom Observation* by Stubbs and Delamont

BBC Hulton Picture Library for the photograph on page 70

The Centre for British Teachers for the photograph on page 48.

Introduction

In recent years there have been a number of exciting developments in language teaching. These developments are sometimes referred to as communicative language teaching or CLT. This book examines how these ideas can be applied to large classes.

What is Communicative Language Teaching?

Communicative Language Teaching means slightly different things to different people and there has been a lot of writing on the theory behind it, (see suggestions for further reading on page 7). In practical terms CLT has had a profound effect on classroom materials and practice. The most important of which has been a greater emphasis on:

- relating the language we teach to the way in which English is used (i.e. an emphasis on *use* rather than *usage* or *form*, see Widdowson 1972)
- activities in which students have the chance to determine what they want to say independently of the teacher (fluency activities)
- exposing students to examples of natural language rather than material which has been written for language teaching purposes (authenticity).

Fluency is a central concept in CLT. It refers to natural language use whether or not it results in native-speaker-like language comprehension or production. A fluency activity is one in which the students are put into a situation where they must use all the language resources they have as effectively as possible. Brumfit (1984:80) gives the following example of a fluency activity:

> The teacher (a Spanish teacher of English in Spain) acts out with one of her students a brief dialogue which she has set up about buying a railway ticket to go to Barcelona. This is done at natural pace, once only. She then tells the class to divide into groups of three and to reconstruct the dialogue. The instruction is given in English, and no further help is offered. The groups, in their second year of English, get out of their seats, divide, and, with great animation, argue about what has happened, much of the argument taking place in English, and construct a dialogue which two members perform, covering more or

less the same meaning as the original but with improvised language, since they cannot possibly remember the form of the English of the original. The teacher goes round the groups, listening and encouraging, and never herself using Spanish. At the end of the lesson, with much laughter, several versions are shown to the rest of the class, all of them in reasonable English, and none very far from the meaning of the original, about which there had been much argument in the groups.

Fluency can be contrasted with accuracy which, as the name implies, is the traditional concern with correctness and formal grammatical usage. There is a place for accuracy work in CLT, although the emphasis is now on use rather than form. The main arguments in favour of fluency activities are:
- they provide opportunities for students to acquire or pick up language (see Brumfit 1984, Littlewood 1984)
- they give students the type of practice they need to learn to communicate effectively outside the classroom context.

Some characteristics of communicative activities

Fluency needs to be developed through activities where:
- students get the chance to be creative and express their own attitudes, feelings, emotions, fears etc., (not what someone else tells them to do)
- students concentrate on 'what' they are saying (or writing) rather than 'how' they are saying (or writing) it, (i.e. the focus is on meaning of the message rather than accuracy of expression)
- students get practice in adjusting to the demands of the situation – in speech this means that the activity must allow for the improvising, paraphrasing, self-correction and unpredictability that is typical of natural language use outside the classroom.

Fluency is most likely to occur with tasks where:
- language is a means to an end, (i.e. students have to achieve something through the use of English. This may be linguistic, e.g. the dialogue creation activity described on page 1, or non-linguistic, e.g. making a kite from a set of written instructions). This emphasis on language being used for a purpose is referred to as task-based learning.
- students have a desire to communicate. This means there must be a 'gap' which students have to bridge by information exchange or negotiation. This may be:
  1 an information gap where a student may have a piece of information which the other student does not have

2 an opinion gap on some issue of concern
3 an affect gap where students exchange feelings and emotions
4 a reason gap where students justify the action they took.

- there is a minimum of teacher intervention. Intervention and frequent error correction interrupt natural language use and distract from the message. CLT is characterised by greater tolerance of error (see Norrish 1983, Revell 1979). It is possible however for the teacher to take part as a co-communicator.

Examples of communicative activities and a further discussion of the principles behind them will be found in Chapters 4, 5 and 6.

Communicative classroom interaction

The growth of CLT has led to important changes of emphasis in the methodology of language teaching. For the purposes of this handbook the most important of these has been the use of pair and group work to stimulate natural language activity in the classroom and the development of new materials and activities.

The use of pair and group work in CLT allows for genuine information exchange and provides opportunities for practice which may not otherwise be available to students who are not living in an English speaking environment. However, the use of pair and group work should not be equated with CLT. Pair and group work can be used as a means of increasing the effectiveness and intensity of accuracy work. This example from Brumfit (1984:79) serves as an illustration of this:

Students in pairs, threes or fours prepare an exercise on a structural item (the first conditional) to which they have just been introduced for the first time. The exercise involves filling in blanks, and they read out the answers in rotation. Later, after some oral preparation, they will be expected to write individually.

Such activities can help familiarise students with working in pairs or groups and prepare the way for genuine communicative methodology in which pair and group work forms an integral part. The introduction of such work is one of the main concerns of the first part of this book.

Communicative materials and activities

There has also been a steady increase in materials and activities which focus on fluency and communication. Many of these have been devised for use with small classes of adults, and the introduction of these materials along with the appropriate methodology has been relatively painless. These same ideas can be adopted or adapted by teachers of large classes in schools or universities and the way this can be achieved is the subject of the rest of this book.

What is a large class?

This book is about teaching English in large classes, but what is a large class? The answer varies. Teachers who are used to groups of 12–14 students might find a group of 20 to be rather threatening. Others may be relieved when they have only 40. Large classes are often found at secondary level but we have seen very large classes of several hundred students in a university. This book is particularly relevant to you if you are teaching or are about to teach in what you consider to be a large class.

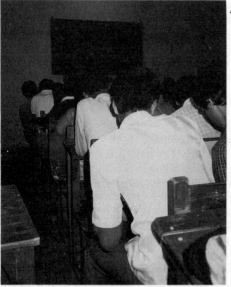

A large class?

Task 1 (For teachers without experience of teaching in a large class)
Look at the photograph of a typical large class. What problems would you expect in using group work in that classroom? What ideas do you have for coping with the problems? If possible, discuss your ideas with a colleague.

Task 2 (For teachers with experience of a large class situation)
Look at this list of problems that a group of teachers felt they encountered when they tried to introduce pair and group work into a large class.

1 The students are not interested when I try things they are unfamiliar with.
2 Discipline is a problem.
3 There are too many physical constraints, such as the rows of desks which are screwed to the floor.
4 It is virtually impossible to provide the necessary duplicated materials.
5 Students prefer grammar and exam practice.
6 The school 'administration' and the teachers in the other classes do not like the noise when all the students talk at the same time.
7 Students will not use English when they are put into pairs and groups.
8 The students complain that I am not teaching them if I ask them to work in pairs and groups.
9 Once motivated by more interesting classroom activities the students become over-enthusiastic and difficult to control.

If possible, discuss each of these with a colleague. From your experience decide on three points that you think represent the most important blocks to success and list any ideas you have for coping with them. (NB Your ideas should be practical and cost little or no money.)

Commentary
In a large class such as the one illustrated on page 4 it would be unrealistic to expect more than a blackboard and a supply of chalk. The rows of heavy desks would be a constraint on group work and management problems might include:
- coping with the noise
- persuading the class to use English
- managing the introduction and setting up of activities
- making limited resources go a long way
- monitoring the work of individuals within the class.

When teachers are faced with problems such as these, or the ones in the list of reported problems, it is not surprising if they feel that there is a gap between the theory of communicative methodology and the reality of their own teaching situation. While many of these problems are real enough, we prefer to look at them as challenges rather than impediments to action, and ideas for solutions will be followed up in subsequent chapters. Compare your ideas with the ones in this book when you reach the relevant sections.

Confidence and conviction

Confidence and conviction are vital ingredients for the successful introduction of change. Any hesitancy or tentativeness on your part spreads to
the students. So, make sure that you are convinced of the value of a
communicative approach and familiar with its techniques before you
introduce more communicative activities into your language classroom. Of
course, everything will not always work the first time, but make sure you
always convey total faith in what you are doing to your students and show
them you feel it is worth trying something more than once.

How this book can help

We believe that a systematic approach to classroom management is vital
for effective teaching. Control is essential for any teaching style in the
large class. For this reason we have taken a step by step approach and
started with fundamental principles of classroom management rather than
with a series of ideas and techniques for communicative language
teaching.

Chapter 1   deals with getting to know your students and the system you
are working in.

Chapter 2   looks at how to create a positive working environment by
establishing routines and developing good instructions.

Chapter 3   examines how to successfully introduce pair and group work
by a process of learner development.

Chapter 4   discusses the principles for exploiting and adapting materials
for large class use.

Chapter 5   presents ideas for coping with limited resources and the
physical problems of the large class.

Chapter 6   presents a way forward for teachers who have successfully
introduced communicative activities.

At the end of each chapter there are consolidation tasks and suggestions
for further reading.

We believe that a considered application of the management advice
given in this book, as well as an appreciation of the underlying principles,
will lead to success in introducing new techniques. From our experience
this should mean increased professional satisfaction for you as well as
greater progress for your students.

Further reading

There has been a wealth of writing on communicative language teaching. The most accessible introductions are Revell 1979, Littlewood 1981, Harmer 1982 and 1983, and Richards and Rogers 1986. See also H G Widdowson *The teaching of English as communication* ELT Journal 27.7.

1 A starting point

One of the biggest problems in starting a new teaching post is the insecurity and uncertainty caused by unfamiliarity with aspects of the job with which all your colleagues and students are totally familiar. Even the most helpful colleagues will omit to pass on certain vital bits of information about the nature of the work or school regulations, simply because they take so much for granted. This is especially true if you are a newcomer to the system as well as to the school. However, if you wish to initiate change and introduce a new approach you need to be confident and authoritative. You can only achieve this if you know the students and the system.

1.1 Finding out about the system

Task 1
Think of an education system with which you are intimately familiar. Imagine that you have been asked to give a foreign teacher who has come to work with you all the information needed to do the job well and appear knowledgeable and confident in front of the students. What would you say under the following headings:
- The administration of the school – who is who
- Departments and how they work
- Class administration and other bureaucracy
- The staffroom and how it functions
- Staff meetings – how often, purpose, procedures
- Internal tests and examinations – where, when and how
- External examinations – when, where, how, who sets them, who marks them
- The system for students who fail in any one year
- Ministry syllabus and guidelines on teaching particular subjects
- The textbooks – who chooses, who buys, how much must be covered
- Marks and reports – systems, procedures and guidelines
- Discipline – sanctions, procedures, responsibility, expectations
- Student representatives – rights and duties (if any)
- Student expectations – methodology, discipline, teacher's role
- Others – (please specify)

Now imagine that you have just started work in a new context. Look at the list again and try to decide what you would like to find out about first, and what you would leave until later. How many different ways can you suggest for finding the information you want? How would you formulate your questions to get the exact information you want? How would you record the information you receive? If possible, discuss your findings for this task with a colleague.

Commentary
Obviously, there can be no set answers to the above task. It merely serves to illustrate the extent of the task for both the person seeking and the person giving the information. However this kind of background information is crucial to the sections which follow. If you are already familiar with the education system and school you are working in, it is worth trying to spell out what you might otherwise take for granted. This is a way of helping yourself and any new colleagues who may ask you for advice. If you are new to the system then make sure you get information under all the headings above as soon as you can.

1.2 Learning names

It is always very important to find out about your students and the first step in this process is learning names. Some teachers may find this difficult in large classes because there are so many students. Fortunately, there are techniques to help you and although learning names can be a lengthy task it should be tackled from the first day. Observation has shown that a teacher's inaccurate use of, or failure to use students' names has a direct correlation with inattention and discipline problems. Knowing the students' names allows you to nominate students with confidence as well as to identify troublemakers. It also indicates that you care about what the students are doing and this helps to contribute to a positive learning environment. It does not matter how you go about learning names as long as you do it efficiently and put them to use quickly. Here are some ways of tackling the problem; a combination of techniques that suits your own way of learning is possibly the most useful.
- Copy out class lists into your record and mark books to gain familiarity with the names.
- Keep a copy of the class list in a plastic envelope as a portable aide-memoire.

- Insist that students sit in the same places and make a seating plan which you can refer to constantly during the lesson. This will help you use names.

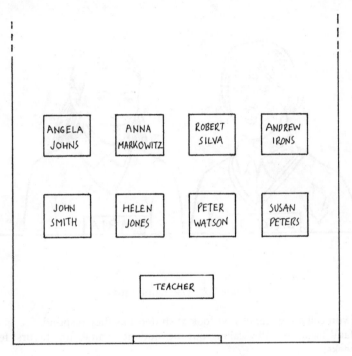

Figure 1.1 Make a seating plan

- Make, or even better, get students to make, name cards on folded sheets of paper or card which are then displayed in front of the students throughout the lesson. You may wish to collect these name cards at the end of each lesson and issue them again at the beginning of the next lesson, one by one. This is a useful test of your memory and students enjoy it if it is done quickly. If you have to fill in a register any cards which are left will clearly indicate who is absent. In some countries students may swap cards to confuse new teachers! If you wish to avoid this you could get students to stick a passport photograph on their cards.

Figure 1.2 Use name cards

- If you call a register always look at students as they respond.
- Hand back books by calling out the students' names for the first few weeks.
- Remember that nobody likes to have their name pronounced badly, so if you are not sure you should check the pronunciation of names on the class list *before* going into class for the first time. Write a phonetic transcription against the more difficult ones if necessary, and practise any that are likely to leave you tongue-tied or embarrassed. When you are ready, practise the pronunciation of names in class, checking with students that you are getting their names right.
- If you are teaching a newly formed class where the students do not know each other try a name learning game. This is an example of an introductory game which is suitable for large classes because it gives you a lot of control. Other introductory games can be found in Revell 1979, Frank and Rinvolucri 1983, Nolasco and Arthur 1987.

NAME BINGO

Aim   Introductory name learning activity
Level Beginner/Elementary/Intermediate

Procedure
1 Start by practising name learning in the usual way. 'Hello, my name's . . . What's your name?' etc.
2 Tell students they must try to remember as many names as possible during the next practice phase.
3 Continue the practice making sure you ask every student at least once.
4 Give out a blank seating plan of the class or put one on the blackboard for students to copy. Ask students to complete it with as many names as they can remember. (This takes about five minutes and cheating is not serious as long as it is not disruptive.)
5 The object of the next stage is for one student to try and name everyone in the class with the aid of his/her plan, and using 'His name's . . .'. 'Her name's . . .'. Start by nominating a student who feels he/she has most/all of the names to begin with. As soon as a student makes a mistake he/she has to sit down and another student is nominated or volunteers. Students may add to their plans during this phase.
6 The winner is the student who gets through all the names without a mistake. As the game progresses more and more students should feel able to name everybody. The game can go on as long as students are motivated to continue, and students can try to name the other students without the aid of the plan if they wish.
7 In order to underline the seriousness of the game, and your own intention of learning names, you must take a turn. One option is to go last.

1.3 Getting to know the students

Name learning is only the first stage in a process of getting to know individual students and their needs. There are a variety of ways in which you can find out more about the people that you teach. These can range from the gathering of information through formal mechanisms such as questionnaires, to very informal methods such as a chat in the corridor. The opening few minutes of a lesson also provide an excellent opportunity for developing social relationships. As the teacher you can initiate exchanges with remarks such as:

'Did you have a good weekend?'

'That's a nice new shirt. Was it a present?' etc.

This is useful language practice and a good example of natural communication between teacher and students. Your main objective is to create a positive working environment, so choose your questions carefully and never make it an inquisition if students are reluctant to answer. Whatever method you use will, however, depend on the circumstances in which you work.

Task 2

You have been asked to teach a group of 45 students in their third and final year of English in a secondary school. Their ages range from 18 to 22; some of the girls are married. At the end of the school year they will take their final exam. You know that six students are repeating the year, having failed in two or more subjects during the previous year. For some this included English, for the others not. Your first impressions of the class suggest that the ability range is very wide – some of the students seem very competent and capable in English, while others seem to know very little English and find writing even simple things laborious. Which of the following methods would you employ to find out more about the students and their needs? What would you consider to be the advantages and disadvantages in each case? Would you use more than one? If so, when and why? You may modify the ideas if you wish.

1   Ask all the students to fill in a simple record card under the following headings.

```
NAME:
DATE OF BIRTH:
MY FAMILY:
WHAT I WANT TO DO WHEN I LEAVE SCHOOL:
SUBJECTS I LIKE AT SCHOOL:
SUBJECTS I DON'T LIKE AT SCHOOL:
I LIKE/DON'T LIKE ENGLISH BECAUSE:
```

Figure 1.3

2   Ask students to write a free essay entitled 'My ambitions'.
3   Give the students a test which includes a selection of grammar points from the previous year and some reading comprehension.
4   Give the students a test which resembles the forthcoming end of year exam.
5   Ask students to complete a questionnaire in English or the mother tongue.

LANGUAGE LEARNING QUESTIONNAIRE

Section A   Tick the option that applies to you.

I want to learn English because:

I want to live and work abroad.	.....
I want to work with English speaking people.	.....
I need to pass my exams.	.....
I need it to get a job.	.....
I like the language.	.....
I can use it in the family business.	.....
I want to learn/understand/sing pop songs.	.....
Other (please specify).	.....

Section B   Tick the option that applies to you.

Which of the following do you want to be able to do in English?

Read English newspapers and magazines.	.....
Read English literature.	.....
Have conversations.	.....
Know the grammar.	.....
Listen to lectures and make notes.	.....
Write to friends.	.....
Write business letters.	.....
Write reports.	.....
Give speeches and talks.	.....
Read science books.	.....
Other (please specify).	.....

Which of the following classroom activities do you think help you to learn and to improve your English? Number them 1, 2, 3 etc., in order of importance to you.

Reading authentic texts (e.g. newspaper articles) with the teacher's help. .....

Repeating what the teacher says. .....

Answering the teacher's questions. .....

Doing oral work in pairs. .....

Group discussion. .....

Doing grammar exercises. .....

Listening to cassette recordings. .....

Self study sessions. .....

Writing compositions. .....

Copying from the board. .....

Learning new words with a dictionary. .....

Other (please specify). .....

6 Hold a discussion in class about the advantages and disadvantages of learning English, the best ways to learn, what students want to learn English for, etc.

7 Determine to hold a five minute interview with each student during the first term.

8 Present a plan for a term's work to the students. Get them to discuss it in groups and come up with suggestions for amendments or additions.

If possible try to discuss your decisions with a colleague. Now compare your ideas with those below.

Commentary

All of the ideas listed have certain advantages when trying to discover more about one's students. However, in a context such as the one above the key questions are:

• Which approach would be readily accepted?
• Which techniques would be easy to manage and implement?
• Which techniques would yield useful information?

The following comments should be read with these questions in mind.

1 Record cards

Students in large classes like the one described on page 14 are likely to be familiar with record cards and the use of this technique would be readily accepted. A record card like the one on page 14 would produce useful personal background on the students but it may not reveal much about their ability in English as they would tend to rely largely on tried and tested formulae in their answers. Whatever your purpose, students are likely to perceive any activity involving writing in English as a learning activity and would expect correction and feedback.

2 An open ended essay

An essay like 'My ambitions' would be too difficult for most of the class. The essay would be difficult to mark and it would be demoralising for many to get their work back covered in red ink. The main advantage of an essay is that it would tell quite a lot about the student's ability in a particular skill. However, weaker students take a long time to complete writing tasks and putting them under pressure only makes them do worse. It is preferable for such tasks to be done at home, although there would always be the risk of cheating.

3 A diagnostic test

Most students would be used to the idea of being tested. However, getting the right sort of test ready is not easy. A diagnostic test is usually based on what has been taught and can be used to find gaps in the student's knowledge. This information can be useful in planning a course. However, many diagnostic tests are based on grammatical knowledge, and a performance on a grammar test may tell us little about other areas e.g. oral performance.

4 An achievement or attainment test

An achievement test seeks to measure what students should know after a period of study, though it is not necessarily based on what has been taught. An exam given at the end of a period of study is basically an achievement test, so giving students the equivalent of the final exam would be a demoralising experience at this stage of the year (although practice exams of this kind would need to feature in the teaching programme later in the year.)

Tests normally reveal little about the students as people or language learners, so what is their value? Clearly in a situation where the teacher can determine the curriculum any diagnostic information is useful. However, if conditions are such that the programme cannot be altered, it may be worth reconsidering the value of putting a lot of time and effort into initial testing, as the students' strengths and weaknesses will soon become apparent. (See Harrison 1983 for a discussion of testing.)

5 Questionnaires
Questionnaires can be very useful activities as we will see in Chapter 3. However, in the early stages a questionnaire could well be met with suspicion and insecurity from students who are not used to being consulted, so it would be unwise to try one until a positive teacher/student, student/student relationship has developed. A questionnaire can provide a useful basis for a class discussion or even a personal interview.

6 Class discussions about language learning
Class discussions about learning can be very useful, but not in the initial stages. It is worth having some kind of input e.g. a questionnaire, to focus the discussion. Remember that in a large class discussions of this sort can easily result in a few confident and capable students dominating the others. This then gives the teacher an unrepresentative impression of the overall ability and views of the class.

7 Individual interviews
Individual interviews can be a very useful way of finding out about individual students. However, many students may be unfamiliar with what personal interviews are meant to achieve, so it is important to tell students that the interview is designed to find out about them, their interests and language level. Unfortunately, the numbers, lack of facilities and the need for students to give up time outside of lessons, may make this idea impractical, especially at the start of the course.

8 Presenting a plan of work
Students may well welcome a plan of work if this is presented with conviction and an air of authority, but any attempt to find out what they might think of it would probably result in either silence or chaos. In many cultures it is not usual or acceptable to negotiate a syllabus, and students would become very insecure. This insecurity could easily result in students thinking that the teacher did not know what to teach or how to teach it.

Getting to know your students is not easy but it is an important part of teaching communicatively. You need to know the activities they enjoy and find beneficial, as well as the topics and content which they find interesting, in order to prepare relevant and appropriate tasks. As we will see in Chapter 4 many communicative tasks can be based on the students' interests, so getting to know them is an important part of our preparation.

1.4 Summary

Even in large classes students need to perceive that the teacher is interested in them as individuals. It is therefore very important to start by learning names and finding out what we can cover in the course of normal teaching. As trust and confidence is built up, the use of group discussion techniques, questionnaires etc., becomes possible. Finding out about our students and taking account of the constraints within a system are vital to the introduction of change, as we need to know what students are used to in planning the gradual introduction of new ideas.

1.5 Consolidation tasks

1 *For teachers new to a system*
  Go through the list of headings on page 9.
  How would you go about getting the information you need?
  Who would you ask?
  Make a list of appropriate questions.
2 Look through the questionnaire on pages 15 and 16 and use it to help you draw up a list of your students' needs and interests as you see them. Try and discuss your list with other colleagues. Interview a few students for their opinion. What conclusions can you come to?
3 How do you learn new words in a foreign language? Do you
  - write them again and again?
  - associate them with something else?
  - remember the circumstances of meeting the word?
  - say them to yourself to remember the sound?
  - visualise their shape?
  - do something else entirely (please specify)?
  Do you use similar strategies when you learn the names of your students? Do you find the suggestions for ways of learning names in this chapter suit your way of learning? If not, list some alternatives.

1.6 Further reading

Vincent 1978 is a very concise and practical introductory handbook which was designed for British volunteer teachers in developing countries. However, it contains useful advice for teachers anywhere and it makes a good starting point. For a further discussion of class profiles see Kennedy and Bolitho 1984, Chapter 2.

2 Creating a productive environment

Effective classroom management is the key to classroom success. Without it students are unlikely to be motivated to continue learning. Before we look at how to introduce communicative activities we need to consider exactly how to create a productive learning environment through efficient management which is achieved by a mixture of common sense and theory.

2.1 Discipline and order

One of the prerequisites for learning is discipline and order. However, any advice on maintaining discipline tends to be platitudinous. Maxims like 'Be firm but fair', 'Have a few reasonable rules and stick to them', 'Show them from the start who's boss', 'Don't smile before December', etc., obviously contain an element of truth, but they are of little practical help to those with problems, as they tell us nothing about the procedures and techniques a teacher might adopt in 'being fair', or in establishing authority. Before examining some of the practical techniques for establishing and maintaining order we need to consider the basis of discipline.

2.2 A positive environment

Discipline and order are often discussed in terms of sanctions e.g. 'I keep my class in if they talk without permission'. It is important however to remember that sanctions are brought into play after a breach of discipline and the key to discipline is the creation of an atmosphere which breeds motivation and cooperation. Such an atmosphere is extremely difficult to characterise except that its absence is immediately apparent to any observer. It is not the product of any particular style of teaching. However, it is unlikely to be present unless everyone has a sense of purpose and knows what is expected of them. Routine is therefore at the very heart of discipline and order.

2.3 Conventions and routines

Task 1

Think critically about your own teaching performance and assess the extent to which you do the following without thinking about them. A score of '1' means that the area of teaching is automatic to you. A score of '5' means that it is something you never do.

1 If possible I prepare the room before the students arrive.   1 2 3 4 5

2 I prepare all the material I need for a lesson, and order and arrange it for quick and easy distribution to groups and individuals.   1 2 3 4 5

3 I teach my group exactly how they are to move into different activities, and they do not do this until they are given the signal.   1 2 3 4 5

4 Whenever I have a new class I train them in how they should attract attention.   1 2 3 4 5

5 I have set routines for giving out and collecting written work, worksheets, materials etc.   1 2 3 4 5

6 I make sure that students are engaged in productive activity as soon as they enter the classroom.   1 2 3 4 5

7 Particularly in large classes I have a system of numbering or marking the materials I issue, so that I know exactly who has what if I need to collect the material in again.   1 2 3 4 5

If most of these activities are automatic to you, you are probably a well organised teacher well able to cope with the extra demands placed on you in a large class. All the examples of teaching behaviour in *Task 1*, and others like them are called conventions and routines (Marland 1975). Conventions are rules governing what is considered to be acceptable behaviour in a given social situation (in this case the classroom), and routines are the regularly repeated activities which support these rules. Conventions and routines are important factors in creating a productive working environment and a well organised teacher is a source of confidence and security for the students. In addition, routines also allow for easy class management so that learning can continue unimpeded.

Security and order are essential to change, so if you teach large classes it is well worth examining the procedures you use to see if they minimise disruption. For example:

- Is movement into and out of group work quiet and orderly?
- Can you check quickly if work has been handed in or not?
- Do you give out books and materials in the most efficient way possible?
- Is control and attention sometimes lost as a result of fumbling for papers, unfamiliarity with equipment etc?

Informality may work with small groups, but it is inadvisable in large classes, where minor weaknesses in management, such as fumbling with papers, tend to be magnified, because there is always someone ready to turn temporary inattention into chaos and indiscipline. Even in small groups weaknesses in management can erode confidence in the teacher, so it is important to establish and maintain routines in any classroom. These routines are very personal and it is essential to develop ones that suit your teaching style and situation. The following tips might be adapted to your needs.

ACTIVITY	TIPS
Receiving the students	Try to arrive first. A position near the doorway allows you to establish individual contact with the students as they come in.
Starting the lesson	Engage students in activity as soon as they sit down, e.g. give them their homework to check through; ask them to write the date in their exercise books; set up routine pairwork exchange of greetings etc. An imaginative alternative is to give students short tasks such as crosswords. Initial tasks can be put on the chairs or desks in handout form or written on a particular part of the board before students come in. Get students involved in the start of the day routines by giving them responsibilities, (see page 26).
Ending the lesson	Bring the lesson to an end before the bell. A summing up and writing of the instructions for the day's homework, or a brief summary

of the day's language point, helps bring a lesson to an orderly close, and contributes to a sense of achievement. With younger students you should always leave the classroom last.

Preparing materials for distribution	Separate different handouts and clip them together, or put them in separate folders. Label them for ease of reference. Count them by rows or groups and put them in the order you wish to distribute them.
Collecting and returning work	Get a student at the front of each row to collect the books. Check that the number in each pile tallies with the number of students in the row as you collect the piles from the front desks. Placing marked books on the desks according to the seating plan before students come in is one way of minimising disruption and gives students something to look at as soon as they come in.
Getting materials back	Number anything you wish to collect in again (e.g. readers or reusable handouts) and allocate a number to each student so you know exactly who has what. You will need plenty of lists or preferably a record book, (see page 114 for an example).
Training students to answer	Insist that students attract your attention by raising their hands. Ignore shouting out and finger snapping. Refuse to proceed with the lesson if this persists. Always wait for silence before speaking once the lesson is in progress.
Moving students into groups	Give instructions for the task in stages. Always check understanding of the instructions by asking students to demonstrate. Name each group, e.g. Group A, and make sure students know what group they are in by asking them to say the relevant letter. Move the members of Group A into position first. The other groups should follow when you give the signal.

2.4 Developing responsibility

Task 2

Look at this list of some of the activities that are carried out in a language classroom.

   handing out papers
   using visual aids
   forming groups
   deciding on breaks
   changing activities
   allocating turns to speak
   creating the learning environment
   choosing materials
   giving feedback
   maintaining discipline
   giving praise
   moving furniture
   deciding what to teach
   planning a series of lessons
   writing on the board

Now decide which ones are:

a) the responsibility of the teacher
b) the responsibility of the students
c) the responsibility of both

If possible discuss your answers with a colleague before reading the next section.

Commentary

The way you answered the questions is a reflection of your view of teaching. If you think that everything on the list is the sole responsibility of the teacher, you are working too hard!

Figure 2.1   'Don't kill yourself with work . . .

Obviously what we can do depends on the age and experience of the students, but systematically involving students in every aspect of classroom management is a way of increasing student involvement. Involvement is important for the maintenance of discipline and helps develop the responsibility needed to make communicative language learning a success. In some areas, e.g. giving out materials, students can be involved from the start. In other areas, e.g. planning work, extended learner training may be required (see Chapter 3). However, increased responsibility does not develop automatically. If you are committed to teaching communicatively you should seek every opportunity to make students more responsible for their own learning from the very first meeting with a class. Here are some ideas which can be introduced without much preparation.

- Make students responsible for routines, such as writing the date on the board.
- Encourage students to clean the board. This is less likely to be regarded as a chore if it is in the context of a campaign to keep the classroom clean and tidy. Make students responsible for developing their own working environment. This might include bringing in posters and decorating the classroom, (see page 97).
- Give students specific areas of responsibility, such as keeping the chalk. Making individual students responsible for distributing or collecting books and material is an effective way of getting these tasks done quickly. Younger students may also enjoy keeping a weather chart, setting up a noticeboard or keeping class library records. These activities involve students and increase the opportunity of genuine communication through writing.
- Involve students in correction and evaluation by using peer correction techniques, (see page 105).

2.5 Instructions

Poor instructions are a major source of problems in any teaching situation, in that they leave the student confused and uncertain. In large classes the problem is magnified because once the students have embarked on a task it is very difficult to rectify any misunderstandings. If you try to talk while the students are working most of them will not listen or hear. If you stop everyone just as they are getting involved it will cause frustration and lack of faith in your ability to organise, especially if this happens often. If you try and repair the misunderstandings group by group the last groups will be totally lost and confused by the time you reach them. There is therefore no acceptable alternative to getting the instructions right the first time.

Task 3
Assess your own instruction-giving with the help of this checklist. Tick the option that applies to you.

		Always	*Sometimes*	*Never*
1	Do you think your instructions through from the point of view of the student, at the planning stage of the lesson?	.....	.....	.....
2	Do you insist on absolute silence and attention from every student before you start giving instructions?	.....	.....	.....
3	Do you stand where you can be clearly seen by all the students when giving instructions?	.....	.....	.....
4	Do you stage your instructions and make sure that students are following each stage as you go along?	.....	.....	.....
5	Do you support instructions with pictures, demonstrations and gestures wherever possible?	.....	.....	.....
6	Do you give instructions in a clear, firm, businesslike voice?	.....	.....	.....

7   If you write instructions
    on the board do you
    insist on full attention
    first and get students
    either to read them out
    aloud or copy them
    down, whichever is
    more appropriate?   ....

8   Do you make it clear
    when students can start?   ....

9   Do you maintain eye   ....
    contact with the whole
    class while you are
    giving instructions?

10 Do you check that your   ....
    instructions have been
    understood before
    allowing students to
    start?

11 Do you check   ....
    understanding by asking
    'Do you understand?'?

12 When a task is very
    complex or unfamiliar
    do you ask some of the
    students to show the
    others what is expected
    of them before they
    start?   ....

13 Do you present the task
    in a different way if it is
    clear that the students
    have not understood?   ....

14 Do you try to repair
    misunderstandings of
    the instructions while
    the activity is in
    progress?   ....

| 15 | Do you monitor yourself to make sure that you are using language the students can understand? | ..... | ..... | ..... |
| 16 | Do you give lengthy explanations? | ..... | ..... | ..... |

Commentary

Getting instructions right is an art. All of the behaviour in the checklist above is desirable except for giving lengthy explanations (No 16), asking 'Do you understand?' to check understanding (No 11) and trying to repair any misunderstandings while an activity is in progress (No 14). The answer to 'Do you understand?', whether 'Yes' or 'No', proves very little, and it is far more revealing if the teacher asks for a demonstration, or for the answer to a question which actually proves understanding. Repairing misunderstandings while an activity is in progress is inadvisable for the reasons stated earlier. If, in spite of all efforts, misunderstandings do occur the only viable solution is to stop everyone and start again, even if this risks frustration for some. Getting one of the students to demonstrate is one way of clearing up misunderstandings quickly and efficiently. Above all, avoid the temptation to explain at length. It is quite easy to use very complicated language which will be difficult to follow. Clear instructions rarely need further explanation and if you adopt the behaviour recommended here you will go a long way towards giving good instructions.

2.6 Other considerations for instructions

In long and complicated tasks it is worth breaking the task up into stages so that students only get the instructions they need for each stage when they need them. This is because it can be very difficult to retain information which is not needed immediately.

Even some relatively simple tasks can be very difficult to explain so it is always worth considering whether demonstration may work better than lengthy instructions given in advance.

Finally, consider the nature of the task itself. Some tasks can only be understood once you start doing them and there is a risk of misunderstanding if the teacher tries to explain everything first. In small group teaching it is relatively easy to sort out misunderstandings while students are doing the task. As we have emphasised, this can be a risky strategy in large classes so it is always important to give careful consideration to the ease with which you can set up a particular task before deciding to use it.

An observation task: instructions

Instruction-giving is such an important factor in the introduction of communicative techniques that it is worth working on this aspect of your performance. Check your performance regularly by recording a lesson or by asking a colleague to sit in on your lesson occasionally. Use this observation task to help you discuss your lesson.

APPRAISAL OF INSTRUCTION GIVING

Put a ring around the number that corresponds to your view of the teacher's performance. '7' is outstanding, '1' is very weak.

Teacher performance	*Weak*			*OK*			*Good*	
1 The teacher was able to obtain the attention of all the students.	1	2	3	4	5		6	7
2 The voice was clear and easy to understand.	1	2	3	4	5		6	7
3 The instructions were staged and easy to follow.	1	2	3	4	5		6	7
4 The instructions were presented in a logical order.	1	2	3	4	5		6	7
5 The instructions were brief and to the point.	1	2	3	4	5		6	7
6 Each stage was clearly indicated and students were told exactly what they had to do and when.	1	2	3	4	5		6	7
7 Any written instructions were easy to read.	1	2	3	4	5		6	7

| 8 | Understanding was effectively checked. | 1 2 3 | 4 5 | 6 7 |

| 9 | The manner was reassuring and students could ask questions if they wanted to. | 1 2 3 | 4 5 | 6 7 |

| 10 | The language of the instruction, was at the right level for the students. | 1 2 3 | 4 5 | 6 7 |

Student performance
Most of the students:
a) listened attentively   Yes .....   No .....
b) did what was required of them   Yes .....   No .....
c) understood without the need
for further explanation.   Yes .....   No .....

Did the students check
understanding with:
a) the teacher?   Yes .....   No .....
b) each other?   Yes .....   No .....

Did any of the students use the
mother tongue?   Yes .....   No .....

Instructions to the observer
1 Observe the way your colleague gives instructions and complete the observation sheet.
2 Ask the teacher you have observed to comment on his/her performance.
3 Give your colleague the completed observation sheet and allow him/her to comment on your observations. See if you reach agreement.
4 Discuss this question:
  If you were to repeat the activities would you change your approach to the instructions? How?

Self or peer observation is an important part of teacher development and observation sheets can help you to focus on desirable teaching behaviour. The task above was constructed during a workshop on micro-teaching in the Sudan and based on Brown 1975. Further ideas and references can be found in Chapter 6.

2.7   Instructions in the mother tongue

Using the mother tongue
Some teachers of English think that using the mother tongue is an effective way of getting over the problem of complicated instructions and misunderstandings. This can be useful if everything else fails but recent research evidence has highlighted the importance of using the target language for classroom management. (See *CILT Guidelines*). The research shows that the use of the mother tongue for instructions removes the greatest single source of genuine communication in the language classroom and students can learn a lot by being asked to listen and do (oral instructions) or read and do (written instructions).

A bilingual approach
It is possible to use a bilingual approach in order to promote student security while you work towards using the target language. In this approach you start by using the mother tongue in order to establish appropriate routines. As soon as this has been achieved you use the target language with the mother tongue as back-up before insisting on the target language only. There is some loss, in terms of opportunities for communication, at the start but the process can be quite efficient and students will adjust to the use of the target language in due course. This is preferable to always giving the instructions in English followed by a parallel version in the mother tongue as there is little motivation for the students to listen to the first version when they know there is an easier one to follow.

Interpreting written or spoken instructions is a useful learning activity and student interest in more communicative activities can be used to promote this, so try to use English as much as possible. If you are unfamiliar with classroom English consult Hughes 1981 and Willis 1981, which give many useful and authentic expressions.

2.8   Increasing student involvement

For control to be maintained it is vital that students remain involved during lessons. One way to create involvement is through a process of individualisation. However, this takes time to achieve, especially in large classes. We will look at some ideas for individualisation in Chapters 4 and 5 but it is a lot easier to introduce such an approach if traditional methods to increase involvement are used from the start. Although the following techniques are not communicative as such, they do help to create a positive working environment. Here are some ideas.

Questioning

Question and answer work remains a widely used technique but when this is used in the large class it is important to keep everyone awake and busy by rapid questioning. The selection of students during such questioning should *appear* to be completely at random, to help keep people 'on their toes' and you should make sure that you cover the whole classroom.

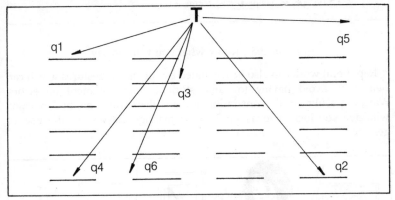

Figure 2.2   Vary your question patterns

Ask the question before appointing a student to answer so that everyone listens to the question in case they are asked to answer, i.e.
'What's the capital of Ireland, Manuel?'
rather than
'Maria, how do you spell Dublin?'

If you see students who are obviously losing interest, attract their attention and direct a question at them. Come back to them again shortly afterwards so that they cannot opt out.

To maintain brisk questioning it is often useful to script the questions at the lesson planning stage. This saves you searching for ideas on the spot and leaves you free to concentrate on what the students are doing and how they are responding.

Level: Upper Intermediate

Objective: To enable the students to talk about changed plans and intentions
and make excuses using: I was going to + but + <u>simple past</u>

Scene setting: Show page of calendar: 31st December
- what day is this?
- what happens in your country?
- what do people do?

In England many people make <u>new year resolutions</u> – repeat –
- do you make them?
- do you keep them?

Presentation: Last year I made lots of resolutions but I have problems.
- I've got no <u>willpower</u> – repeat –

Figure 2.3   Know what you want to say

Rapid oral work can also be facilitated by the use of gestures which can help you avoid having to name students and comment on errors. Watching a film or demonstration of the 'silent way' method in action will give you lots of ideas on how to manage classes by the use of gesture.

Figure 2.4   Use gesture

Another way of increasing student involvement during periods of question and answer work is to follow up answers with questions like 'Is she right?', 'Do you agree?' etc. This encourages other students to listen and involves them in the process of evaluation.

Finally, in a large class it is vital that students only respond with the teacher's permission. However, standing up to answer can seriously hinder rapid oral work so if your students are used to this you may wish to introduce new rules. In some classes you may wish to insist that students put their hands up to answer. In others it may be enough to nod in the direction of the student who wants to speak. Do not allow yourself to be swayed from the procedure you choose because the students seem enthusiastic. Over-enthusiasm can be just as much a cause of disruption and lack of control as boredom.

Repetition

Rapid repetition of a model sentence or of a response to a prompt given by the teacher, or another student, by small groups of students in turn helps the teacher get round a large class quickly, e.g.

Teacher:	He works in Madrid. Jose.
Jose:	He works in Madrid.
Teacher:	(Nods to Carmen)
Carmen:	He works in Madrid.
Teacher:	Alonso. etc.

It can be made more interesting if the class is asked to concentrate on getting the rhythm, stress and intonation right; repetition can help give students the confidence to get their tongues around English sounds if they are given adequate support and not asked to repeat too much, too soon. However, remember that repetition is mechanical and has its limitations, so try to introduce pair work as soon as possible, (see page 42).

Management of lesson time and pace

The attention span among most students, especially younger ones, can be very short so it is important to plan frequent changes of focus or activity within a lesson. Allocate time limits for each activity when you are planning the lesson and avoid the temptation to let activities carry on until the students are bored. All the activities should be sufficiently challenging to keep the students interested for a reasonable length of time. This is especially true if you want to circulate and listen to students during pair work. If the task requires little more than the creation of two or three sentences, the students will have finished and become bored by the time you have listened to two or three pairs. In the early stages when pair work exchanges are necessarily short you should insist on short, sharp practice spots. The pace can be maintained by ostentatious time-keeping with a stop-watch, or a wristwatch or clock with a seconds hand. It is also important that students start and stop at the same time and devices such as 'Go' and 'Stop' traffic lights signs can help to convey a sense of urgency.

2.9 Summary

The advice in this chapter relates to basic management skills. Being in command of one's classroom means being aware of and controlling what is going on at all times. This presupposes:
1 an ability and willingness to organise and manage every part of every lesson
2 a determination to set up routines and recognisable methods of working.
These traditional virtues are essential to the creation of the productive learning environment needed to teach communicatively. In the classroom discipline brings freedom.

2.10 Consolidation tasks

1 Read this description of a teaching problem.

You have just taken over a new group of 14–15 year olds from a teacher who is on leave. The teacher on leave is very popular with the students. Your school has a special room for English. You find the class has been used to coming into the room and finding their own places. The noise from the scraping of chairs and arguments about seats sometimes continues for several minutes after you have come into the classroom and you think this initial noise is having a negative effect on them for the rest of the lesson.

Look back over the section on 'Routines' and decide what you might do to cope with a similar problem. Discuss your solution with a colleague.

2 Look at this list of activities which some teachers use to increase student involvement.
Keeping the chalk

Cleaning the room
Collecting and distributing books
Keeping a class noticeboard
Running a class library
Keeping the class register
Organising an English club
Writing on the board
Which activities would you introduce immediately with a new class? Which ones would you introduce after you have got to know the students? How would you involve as many students as possible in each of the tasks listed above?

3 'Classroom instructions are usually best learnt directly' (from Gower & Walters 1983).

A recent beginner's course for young teenagers (Hutchinson 1985) includes a page where classroom instructions are taught with the help of simple visuals. Make a list of the classroom instructions you would want to introduce from the earliest stages. Consider the visuals that you might use to illustrate each instruction. (This will help students keep an 'English only' notebook.)

Figure 2.5   Pick up your pen

2.11   Further reading

Marland 1975 is a classic introduction to classroom management for students on UK teacher training courses. Good advice on management issues for new teachers can be found in Chapter 3 of Gower and Walters 1983. Useful management advice as well as an introduction to classroom English can be found in Willis 1981 and a comprehensive description of the English we use in the classroom in Hughes 1981. Either/both of these last books can be recommended for teachers anxious to improve their knowledge of classroom English.

3   Learner development

In Chapter 2 we concentrated on the need for control. Once this has been established we can begin to broaden and extend the ways in which to engage students in learning English.

3.1   The starting point

As we have suggested, the most important source of discipline is the creation of a classroom regime that breeds motivation and co-operation, because everyone has direction and knows what is expected of them. In large classes students have usually been together for a long time; they are secure with one another and with the conventions governing behaviour in their learning situation. They know how lessons are usually structured and they know what type of questions the teacher will ask as well as how they are expected to answer them. They know roughly what the average teacher will and will not accept, and they will have their own particular perceptions of 'the good teacher' and 'the good lesson'. In other words there is a culture of the classroom which Furlong 1976 describes as:

> What the participants need to know to be able to behave appropriately from minute to minute in changing circumstances.

A teacher who comes in with new ideas or presenting an image which is contrary to the expected norm, or organising lessons differently from what students are used to, will inevitably provoke a reaction from the students. In some cases this may well manifest itself in indiscipline and chaos. This is why the first step in introducing change is to take account of student expectations.

3.2   Student expectations

Students come to lessons with expectations as to what is normal. In a foreign language classroom we can expect the source of these expectations to include:

1 Cultural transmission.

Different societies will have different concepts of the teacher's role, the place of the student, appropriate ways of learning etc.

2 Previous experience of learning and teaching.

English is not the only subject on the curriculum. The methodology which students are used to in other subjects may have an important influence on how far learners can adapt to something new in their English language lessons.

3 Folklore about the nature of language and language learning.

We all have ideas about how languages are learnt and what is important in learning them. Sometimes these ideas are sound. On other occasions they can be a block to effective learning; e.g. many students do not feel they have learnt a new word unless they can have a translation of it. The idea that there may be no mother tongue equivalent for an English word can be very disturbing for some.

4 Ideas as to the status of English.

Do students view English as an academic subject to be studied for an exam or as something which they might use outside the classroom?

The important thing to remember is that the communicative approach to English teaching may be in conflict with the student's view of the educational process as a whole and their perception of their role in it.

3.3 Lockstep

We should always be wary about generalising, but most students in large classes will be used to a style of teaching known as 'lockstep' in which the teacher wholly controls the content, stages and pace of the lesson. In this form of language teaching the teacher typically takes up a position in front of the class and is responsible for controlling who should speak and when. There is usually a considerable amount of teacher input and the pattern of interaction typically consists of:

Teacher initiation:	Is it big or small?
Student reply:	Small.
Teacher evaluation:	Yes, it's small.

If students are used to lockstep it is likely that they will view the teacher as an authority figure and assume that:

1 It is the teacher who must initiate all the language exchanges in the class.

2 It is the student's task to respond to the teacher.

3 The teacher has to judge whether the student's performance is acceptable or not for learning to take place.

3.4 Transmission or communication?

Lockstep has a variety of origins. One of these is the view that it is the
teacher who should be the main source of knowledge and information.
This is sometimes referred to as the 'transmission' model of education
(Barnes 1975). The transmission model sees knowledge as something
which can be passed on as a sort of product. This view of teaching as
'telling' can be contrasted with exploratory learning in which the emphasis
is on the process by which students are able to make ideas their own.
Observers like Barnes argue that students learn better when they get a
chance to talk about and experience what they are learning. This is a view
which can be expressed simply as follows:

I hear and I forget, I see and I remember, I do and I understand.

Although Barnes is mainly concerned with the teaching of other subjects
in the curriculum, especially science, there is a great deal of relevance in
what he says for language teaching. For although lockstep is a valid style
of teaching which is useful for certain language learning activities such as
drilling and controlled practice, it puts the teacher and the students in a
different role from what is required of them in a communicative language
teaching programme. The key point is that if we 'learn by doing' (and
there is a lot of evidence that this is how we effectively learn skills such as
riding a bicycle or swimming as well as language) then the corollary is we
'learn what we do'! Taking part in controlled question and answer practice
does not necessarily help students to use English outside the classroom. If
you are interested in teaching communicatively you must move from
lockstep to a classroom where students get the chance to use English
independently of the teacher. See page 59 for the characteristics of activities which can achieve this.

Task 1

Look at these teacher roles.

Facilitator	someone who makes the learning process easier by devising learning tasks, helping students find sources of information etc.
Consultant	someone who is available to give advice if this is required
Instructor	someone whose role is to pass on information directly

Questioner	someone who makes sure that students have learnt what is required by asking questions
Organiser	someone who makes sure that books, materials etc., are in the right place at the right time
Agent of discipline	someone whose role is to keep order
Provider	someone who issues books and materials
Evaluator	someone who gives students feedback as to what is right and wrong
Setter of social climate	someone who creates the mood and atmosphere of the lesson

Which two roles do you think are most common during group work?
Which two roles are most important in a lockstep class?

Commentary

Research has shown that in group work the teacher was found to act as a consultant and facilitator more than as a questioner and instructor (see Kerry and Sands 1982). While pair and group work can be used for tightly controlled practice, its great advantage is that it gives an opportunity for 'free' activities in which students can determine what they want to say independently of the teacher. Usually teachers do not correct students during such free activities. Teachers may even feel redundant as they walk round listening and storing information for use later in the lesson. It is therefore not surprising that students who are used to the role of the teacher in lockstep may question the value of group work which encourages assumptions which are the opposite of those they are used to. They expect the teacher to 'teach', by which they mean ask questions, explain and evaluate. They are therefore confused when the teacher appears to be doing very little while they are working. This may be one reason why the sudden introduction of 'free activities' may be met with apparent disinterest, lack of participation and in some cases downright hostility. Another reason may be that students do not know how to make use of the opportunities afforded by freer activities because they quite simply do not know what they are expected to do. One solution is to start by asking students to perform familiar controlled activities in pair and group work. When students get used to these it is then possible to introduce freer activities. Learner development refers to the process by which we introduce students to the 'how' and 'why' behind our methodology so that they are able to make full use of the opportunities for learning.

3.5 An approach to learner development

The first step is to find out as much as possible about the students and their background (see pages 10 to 19). This may tell you something about their expectations. Students who have just started English may not have particularly strong views about what they expect from their English teacher although they will be influenced by their previous experience of school learning. Students who have already done some English may have particularly strong views about what is appropriate. It would be ideal to have access to a full and reliable record of work done in English so far, but in practice such records are rarely available in a useful form. Asking the students for information can be revealing, but complaints should never be taken too seriously. The main objective is to get a feel of the activities and control procedures that students are used to and will readily accept so that you have a starting point. In doing this the key questions to bear in mind are:

1   Have the students had any responsibility for working independently of the teacher before?
2   Are the students used to working without immediate teacher feedback?

If the answer is 'no' to either of these questions it is likely that the sudden introduction of pair or group work will cause problems. In a small multi-national group of adults the presence of one or two students who are not used to pair or group work rarely poses a significant management problem although the students concerned may experience considerable distress. In a large school class (which tends to be monolingual) the effect of uncertainty can lead to considerable disruption, so it is important to start with what students are used to. It is therefore vital to introduce pair work gradually and systematically.

3.6 Introducing pair work

If students are used to lockstep, security and control can be promoted by staging the introduction of pair work so that responsibility for determining who should speak is gradually shifted from the teacher to the students. Ways in which this can be done include:

1   Giving some of the responsibility for asking questions to the students.

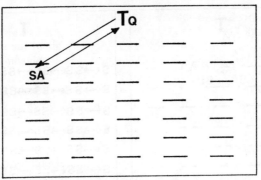

Teacher asks student A a question. A answers

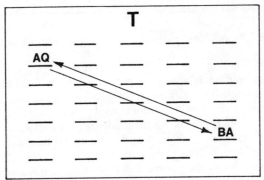

Student A now asks student B the same question

Figure 3.1 Open pairs

a) Write the questions and answers on the board.
b) Ask a student the question (choose one of the better students).
c) The student replies.
d) Point to the question and tell one student, A, to ask another, B.
e) A asks the question and B replies.

This is called open pair work. When students are familiar with open pairs they can be asked to work in adjacent pairs to get them used to working together. Adjacent pair work should however be kept short and snappy as students are less involved than in open pairs because the centre of attention is a small part of the room. Finally, ask students to carry out the same activity for a short period in closed pairs.

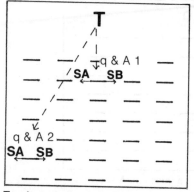

Teacher nominates individual pairs to
ask and answer the questions

Figure 3.2 Adjacent pairs

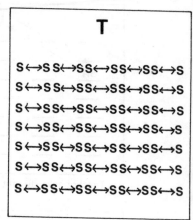

Figure 3.3 Closed pairs

2 Dialogue Reading

Dialogue reading is a way of getting students used to the idea of
speaking English to each other independently of the teacher.
a) Teacher reads part A. Students read part B.
b) Teacher reads part B. All the students read part A.
c) Divide class into halves, A and B, for choral practice.
d) Organise class into pairs. Label each student A or B. Check all
   students know their parts. Tell As to raise hands and then all Bs.
e) Ask the class to practice the dialogue quietly.

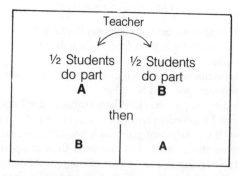

Figure 3.4 Choral practice

Asking students to come out to demonstrate what is expected is another useful way of getting them used to the idea of pair work.

a) Copy an exchange onto the board for the class to follow.

b) Ask two students to come to the front of the class with their books. Tell one of them to be A and the other B. Each one should look at the line of dialogue and make eye contact with the other speaker before saying it as naturally as possible.

At this stage periods of closed pair work should be kept to a maximum of a minute. Gradually extend the period of closed pair work and circulate to check that all the students are practising. Make sure that students change parts regularly so that they get practice in asking and answering questions.

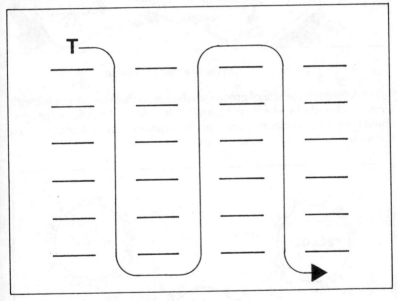

Figure 3.5 Circulate to check work

3.7 Introducing group work

You should follow the same general principles in setting up group work as you did for pair work although you will need to consider the seating very carefully indeed (see pages 81, 82). In setting up groups for the first time it is worth asking one group to demonstrate in front of the class.

Figure 3.6   Organise a demonstration

Think through the size of groups in advance so that you are not left with a couple of students who do not know what to do. In the initial stages you should write the students' names on the board or draw a diagram which shows the composition of the groups.

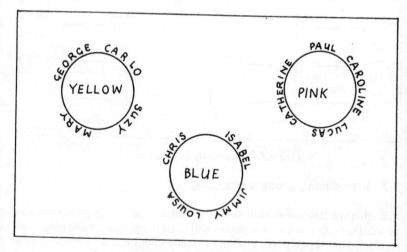

Figure 3.7   Give groups a name

It can help to give groups a name for ease of reference. The names can be used to revise items of vocabulary e.g. colour words or birds, or they can be chosen to add an element of fun to the lesson e.g. by using 'famous' names. It is also very important that everyone knows what they have to say, write or do, so think through the instructions carefully, (see page 27).

One of the biggest problems in the early stages of group work is to make sure that all the learners know what is expected of them without causing them to lose interest in the task. As we suggested earlier the key is to centre the early stages of group work around traditional activities that students are familiar with, such as group preparation of the answers to a series of reading comprehension questions. This will get them used to working together in English without the additional burden of adjusting to a new type of activity or task.

3.8 Managing pair and group work

Students need to adjust to working in groups. On the whole group work works much better after training when students have got used to:

1 starting and stopping when you tell them to
(introduce a special signal such as a series of loud claps and make sure students start and stop when they hear it)
2 switching quickly from one activity to another
(always insist that things are done quickly and promote a constructive atmosphere by keeping students on their toes)
3 working quietly
(tell students they do not have to shout in pair and group work – it is important to keep the level of noise down)
4 listening carefully to instructions
(do not be afraid to stop giving instructions if some students are not listening)

Encourage the students to ask questions if they have any doubts and always check that students are doing the right thing by monitoring pair and group work.

3.9 Monitoring pair and group work

It is important for the teacher to circulate during pair and group work. When you are moving around remember to put yourself in a position where you can see and be seen, and make sure you are not deaf and blind to everyone except the students you are with. It is important that students feel that you are interested and also actively working. However, it is also important not to hover over the students, so either listen at a distance or crouch if you are at close quarters.

Figure 3.8   Monitoring work

When the activity starts go to the students who need firm direction and get them working. Then go to the weakest ones and give them encouragement and help. Finally, circulate amongst all the students and show them that you are listening. If you spot any students who are obviously not performing the task you should go to find out the source of the problem. If necessary give them extra information or direct them to new resources.

Although the aim is to get students used to working without you the majority tend to feel insecure if the teacher does not pay attention to what they are doing. It is important however that students get used to the fact that feedback will be delayed and you should avoid the temptation to overcorrect them during an activity. Note the mistakes made during the activity on a piece of paper and use the information for remedial teaching later. This task is facilitated if you use a feedback sheet to focus on what the students are saying.

Name	Date	Nature of task	Grammar	Vocabulary	Pronounciation and fluency
Mario	16/5	discussion	The thing who was taken	<u>stealer</u>	<u>thick</u>

Figure 3.9

Post lesson feedback alleviates the feeling that many students have that an activity is a waste of time if the teacher does not correct them and reinforces the idea that the teacher remains aware of what they are doing during pair or group work (see page 41, British Council ELTI film notes 1980 and Nolasco and Arthur 1987).

3.10 Introducing communicative activities

Once students have got used to working together on controlled activities such as dialogue reading it is possible to move on to some of the less controlled activities described in Chapter 3 of Revell 1979. As usual however it is very important to stage the introduction of new activities. In order to work out how this can be done we need to consider the notion of a communicative continuum.

3.11 The communicative continuum

A number of observers have suggested that there is a continuum of activities to promote communicative competence, (Harmer 1983, Littlewood 1981).

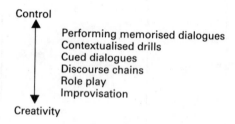

For our purposes the most important difference between these activities is the extent to which the students are responsible for deciding on what they say. In a memorised dialogue, for example, production is based on a model so students have no choice. At the other end of the scale the emphasis is on creativity and an appropriate activity would aim to get students to use all the language they have as fluently as possible and there would be no attempt to determine what they would say.

The activities in the list above centre on verbal communication. It is possible to do the same with other areas of communication. When you finish *Task 2* try to draw a continuum for another skill e.g. writing.

Task 2

Look at these examples of language learning activities and place them on a continuum from control to creativity. The first example has been done for you.

Control ◄————————C————————► Creativity

Activity A

Complete the other part of the dialogue.

Peter: Let's have a drink. Would you like tea or coffee?
You:
Peter: I'll put a record on first. Do you like jazz?
You:

Activity B

Work in pairs and complete the dialogue between A and B.

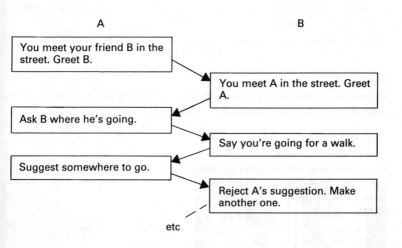

A

> You meet your friend B in the street. Greet B.

B

> You meet A in the street. Greet A.

> Ask B where he's going.

> Say you're going for a walk.

> Suggest somewhere to go.

> Reject A's suggestion. Make another one.

etc

Activity C

Make sentences which are the same as the model.

Teacher: John has written the letter.
Model: John wrote it yesterday.
Teacher: John has seen the film.
Student: John saw it yesterday.

Activity D

Work in pairs and construct a dialogue. Use the cards to help you.

Part A

You wish to buy a car. You are in a showroom looking at a second-hand car that might be suitable. You decide to find out more about it, for example how old it is, who the previous owner was etc. You can pay up to about £900 in cash.

Part B

You are a car salesman. You see a customer looking at a car in the showroom. The car is two years old and belonged to the leader of a local pop group. It does about 20 miles to the gallon. Your firm offers a three month guarantee and can arrange hire purchase. The price you are asking for the car is £1400.

Figure 3.10

Activity E

In groups of four devise a questionnaire and then use it to find out the attitudes of others in your class to keeping fit.

Activity F

Work with a partner. Look at the pictures and decide what order they should be in to tell the story correctly.

Figure 3.11

Activity G

Students have a map in front of them and respond to teacher's questions by looking at the map and giving appropriate answers, e.g.

Teacher: Excuse me, where's the post office?
Student: It's opposite the theatre.
Teacher: Excuse me, where's the bank?
Student: It's next to the cinema.

Activity H

In groups of four discuss ideas for the composition (title on blackboard) and decide on a structure for it.

A suggested solution for this task can be found on page 57. The important thing to remember is that if students are only ever asked to do controlled activities they will be lost if they are suddenly asked to be creative. Stage and grade the presentation of activities so that you build confidence in students by gradually moving from the familiar to the unfamiliar. This process can be summarised as follows:

1   You introduce students to new patterns of classroom interaction. (This can be facilitated by the use of traditional activities.)
2   You gradually introduce more communicative activities.
3   You integrate new ways of working in the classroom with communicative tasks.

This third stage is referred to as communicative language teaching. There are other routes to the same goal. For example, some teachers may prefer to introduce communicative tasks from the start, and in cases where students are not familiar with pair or group work it is possible to adapt these for use with the whole class, or part of a class to start with (see Chapter 4). The approach you adopt will depend on your circumstances, but at each stage you have to consider the amount of support that students need in order to complete an activity or task. In some cases this support may be non-linguistic. For example, in **Activity E** unfamiliarity with the notion of 'keeping fit' or the conventions involved in preparing and using questionnaires may be more of a barrier to the completion of the task than an inability to form questions, and we will look at ways in which we need to adapt activities in Chapter 4.

3.12   The 'why' of learner training

Up till now we have concentrated on how to take part in communicative activities. However, learner security can be promoted if the students know why they are being asked to use English in pair and group work. If you decide to discuss the rationale of what you are doing make sure you avoid aggression or self-justification as this can become counterproductive very quickly. We have found that the idea that language use is developed through use is intuitively satisfying to most students, and therefore the main task is to continually demonstrate ways in which the practice activities contribute to the students' ability to use English for communication. Essentially this is a process whereby the teacher needs to appeal to the students' common sense. Reference to the ways in which the activities can help students outside the classroom as well as discussions based on language learning questionnaires (see page 15) can help, and here the use of the mother tongue is an advantage. It is however very important to make sure that you have established a trusting relationship with the group before attempting any discussions of the 'why' of what you are doing. Unless there is an element of trust students are unlikely to be forthcoming and it is very easy for the teacher to fall into the trap of being defensive.

3.13 Training monolingual classes

Pair and group work can be hampered if students insist on using the mother tongue when they are working independently of the teacher. In some cases the problem is so bad that teachers abandon pair and group work altogether. Fortunately this is not inevitable and it is possible to get monolingual classes to work in English.

The first step is to get students to accept that there is a value in working in English. Most students will agree to this even if they do not always do it! However, once verbal agreement has been obtained it is possible to make a 'contract' so that the students take on the responsibility for maintaining an 'English only' rule in the classroom. Try and establish an air of fun and commitment to speaking English e.g. through a sign on the door saying *You are now entering an English only zone*, and let students enforce the rule. With more mature students you could also try a forfeit system which might involve a small fine. All of these are likely to work better than teacher nagging!

However, although the aim is to get students working in English, it is important to consider why students are using the mother tongue in the first place as this will influence what you decide to do about it. These questions may help:
• Do they find the tasks too difficult?

- Are they using the mother tongue to explain things to each other?
- Do they want to talk about things unconnected with the lesson?
- Do they wish to show lack of enthusiasm for what they have been asked to do?
- Do they become so involved in a task that they forget to use English?
- Do they need a substitute for English words they do not know?
- Do they use the mother tongue because they feel uneasy at using a foreign language with their peers?

The use of the mother tongue to check understanding and provide explanations can be very productive and many students would be very frustrated if they were told not to. It is therefore always worth discussing the advantages and disadvantages of resorting to the mother tongue. Although it is a slightly artificial situation to have to use English with their peers, it is the only source of practice for many students and the advantages should never be lost sight of. It is important to get classes used to working in English from the start and controlled activities, such as dialogue repetition, will help students get over the barrier of having to suddenly speak English to a peer without the additional burden of having to think of something to say.

Success breeds confidence, so take any opportunity to praise students who work in English during pair and group work. If possible write down the good things that individuals say in English to prove that they *can* use English to communicate. It can also be useful to ask or listen for examples of what students say in the mother tongue in order to be able to show that they could have used English instead, if they had put in a little more thought and effort. Students will need a certain amount of classroom English to seek clarification in English, so you should teach expressions like the following from the start.

Please can you tell me . . .
What does X mean?
How do you spell Y?
What is the English for . . .?
Please repeat . . .

The use of the mother tongue might signal frustration because the students perceive the task as being too difficult. It is important not to ask students to do too much too soon. It can be very stressful to work in a foreign language for an extended period, so it is important to keep the initial stages of open-ended pair and group work relatively short.

It is not uncommon for students to get so involved in a task that there is a genuine need to use the most natural and effective means of communication available, which is the mother tongue. This is always a risk. One way to ensure that English is used at some stage is to build in some kind of feedback or report session. If students feel that it is likely that they will have to perform in front of the rest of the class they will tend to prepare for it.

Obviously students are more likely to use English if you avoid using the mother tongue yourself, so make sure you practice what you preach. Willis 1981 and Hughes 1981 are excellent sources for teachers who want to improve the English they need for classroom management. The advantages of using English for classroom communication are well worth the effort for teachers and students. Remember that what goes on in a classroom is largely habit, and you cannot change habits overnight. It is possible to get monolingual groups to work constructively in pairs but do not set your expectations too high at the start. If most of the students use some English you have already done quite well, so persevere and eventually you will be successful.

3.14 Summary

Older students are particularly resistant to change if the change that is required of them runs counter to what is taking place elsewhere in the system. The creation of a fresh set of expectations through a process of learner training is therefore essential to a successful introduction of change. Successful learner development needs to cover the 'how' and the 'why'. This chapter has concentrated on the 'how' and illustrated ways in which the pair and group work which are essential for a successful programme in communicative language teaching can be gradually introduced to students who have not encountered them before. The principle of proceeding from the familiar to the unfamiliar can however be applied to the introduction of any new activities.

3.15 Consolidation tasks

1 Do your students get a chance to speak independently of the teacher. Ask a friend to use this simple observation form to find out. If this is impossible answer the questions as honestly as possible. Choose a lesson where the objective is oral work. Mark the scale with an X to indicate your general impression for your period of observation.

a)	Students spoke when they wanted	⊢─┼─┼─┼─┼─┼─⊣	Teacher determined who should speak
b)	Less than a third of the students spoke	⊢─┼─┼─┼─┼─┼─⊣	More than two-thirds of the students spoke
c)	Teacher moved a lot from the front	⊢─┼─┼─┼─┼─┼─⊣	Teacher hardly moved from the front
d)	There was a lot of student/student interaction in English	⊢─┼─┼─┼─┼─┼─⊣	There was hardly any student/student interaction in English
e)	Most of the students volunteered to answer	⊢─┼─┼─┼─┼─┼─⊣	Less than a third of the students volunteered to answer
f)	Teacher spoke most of the time	⊢─┼─┼─┼─┼─┼─⊣	Students spoke most of the time

Discuss ways in which a teacher can cut down on teacher talking time.

2 Decide on the text for a leaflet entitled *The advantages of pair and group work in English*. The leaflet will be in the students' mother tongue but you can prepare an English version for translation if you prefer. Look at the leaflet critically with the help of the following questions.

- Is the information clearly presented?
- Have you covered all the important areas?
- Is it at the right level for your students?

If possible discuss the leaflet with your colleagues.

(Leaflets of this sort can be a useful part of learner development and you might consider producing a version for classroom use)

3.16 Further reading

Accounts of the characteristics of a good language learner can be found in Rubin 1975 and Naiman 1978. A survey of the work in this area is in Ellis and Sinclair 1988. For an introduction to the view that social interaction is influenced by the perspectives of teachers and pupils see Delamont 1976. Stubbs and Delamont 1976 also contains an interesting article by Nash on pupil's expectations. Relevant articles also appear in *Practical English Teaching* and *Modern English Teacher*.

```
              G
      C  A    B   D  F  H  E
Control ◄───────────────────► Creativity
```

4 Communicative materials in the large class

Much of the communicative material now available was developed for small classes of adult learners. Much less communicative material has been written specifically for large classes of school children and so for many teachers it is either a case of making do with old material or trying to adapt the new. This chapter therefore aims to:

1 Outline how traditional material which is widely available can be made more communicative.
2 Show how some of the more recent methodological suggestions can be made to work in the large class situation.

4.1 Background

If we look at any language teaching material we see that it contains three elements.
- *Data* (this may or may not be linguistic).
- *Information on the language* – or grammar (this is optional).
- *A task* (usually identified by an imperative).

A

> **Say these words**:
> 1 A pipe
> 2 A lighter
> 3 A postcard
> 4 A comb
> 5 A pen
> 6 A sandwich
> 7 A cup of coffee
> 8 An apple
> 9 An orange

From *Contemporary English* by Rossner *et al.*, Macmillan

B

```
Shakespeare L, 8 Birch Ct,Edgcumbe Pk .......Crowthorne 77489
Shakespeare L, 52 Shepherds La ..................Bracknell 48017
Shakespeare Rnld, 32 Burnetts Rd ..................Windsor 5715
Shakir Dr A.K, 95a Stoke Poges La ..................Slough 2892
Shakur A, 3 Eltham Av,Caversham .................Reading 47837
Shaldrake E.T, 27 Larchfield Rd..............Maidenhead 3017
Shale Robt, 17 Southfield Rd,Flackwell Hth.....Bourne End 2549
Shalehall Ltd,Holding Company, Cowarth Park ........Ascot 2514
Shalet Ltd,Curtains—
      109 Friar St ......................................Reading 5078
      12 Queensmere ..................................Slough 2316
Shalibane Ltd,Engs, Gardner Rd .................Maidenhead 2112
Shall H.J, 6 Helmsdale,Crownwood ..............Bracknell 48199
Shallcroft Marketing Services Ltd—
      House on the Creek, Raymead Rd .............Maidenhead 7060
```

Figure 4.1

A is an example of language teaching material, B is not. Why?
B could be suitable language teaching material if an appropriate task were formulated, and it is the relationship between the task and the data which is fundamental, (see Breen, Candlin and Waters 1979).

As a teacher you always need to ask what type of interaction or communication your tasks promote. If you find that the majority of the tasks you use only generate traditional question and answer patterns (see Chapter 3) then you need to introduce more communicative activities.

4.2 Characteristics of communicative activities

The sort of tasks we choose will depend on our view of language teaching but as we saw in the Introduction (page 2) genuinely communicative activities will have the following characteristics.

- They involve using language for a purpose.
- They create a desire to communicate. This means there must be some kind of 'gap' which may be information, opinion, affect or reason which students seek to bridge.
- They encourage students to be creative and contribute their ideas.
- They focus on the message and students concentrate on 'what' they are saying rather than 'how' they are saying it.
- The students work independently of the teacher.
- The students determine what they want to say or write. The activity is not designed to control what the students will say.

A first step is to analyse the materials we are using to see whether they meet the criteria outlined above.

Task 2

Look back at the activities on pages 51 to 53 of Chapter 3 and complete this grid. Put a tick if you think the activity has the characteristics in the column. Put a cross if you think it does not. If you are not sure, put a question mark.

CHARACTERISTICS	ACTIVITIES							
	A	B	C	D	E	F	G	H
Purpose								
Desire to communicate								
Encourages creativity								
Focus on the message								
Promotes independence								
No constraints on what students produce								

Now rank the activities according to how communicative you think each one is. If possible, discuss your work with a colleague before continuing.

Commentary

Some language teaching tasks, such as a mechanical drill (Activity C), meet none of these characteristics. Others, such as the exercise in questionnaire design (Activity E), would potentially meet all of them. Many of the rest fall somewhere along the communicative continuum we discussed in Chapter 3 (page 50). If you are interested in teaching more communicatively you should study the tasks in your textbook with these characteristics in mind. If most of the tasks are mechanical you will need to supplement them. The examples of communicative tasks given in this chapter meet most, if not all, of these criteria. A first step therefore must be for you to become familiar with the communicative activity types which are available. Sources which you might consider include:

- teacher's resource books
- articles from journals
- materials with a focus on communication
- textbooks which incorporate communicative language teaching ideas.

Sources which are particularly useful for teachers in large classes can be found on page 127.

4.3 Exploiting the textbook

A first step towards solving the materials problem is to consider ways in which the textbook you are using can be exploited communicatively. In doing this you should consider whether you can make the content more interesting by introducing new tasks or improving the way in which the material is presented.

4.4 Using a narrative text

In some countries teachers have to build much of a language teaching programme around textbooks which are essentially collections of narrative texts. Fortunately, these texts are a flexible resource which can be used in a variety of ways. Our first example illustrates how a text from *Practice and Progress* could be the stimulus for exercises which provide variety along with varying degrees of control.

---

34 Quick Work

Ted Robinson has been worried all the week. Last Tuesday he received a letter from the local police. In the letter he was asked to call at the station. Ted
5 wondered why he was wanted by the police, but he went to the station yesterday and now he is not worried any more. At the station, he was told by a smiling policeman that his bicycle had
10 been found. Five days ago, the policeman told him, the bicycle was picked up in a small village four hundred miles away. It is now being sent to his home by train. Ted was most surprised
15 when he heard the news. He was amused too, because he never expected the bicycle to be found. It was stolen twenty years ago when Ted was a boy of fifteen!

From *Practice and Progress* by Alexander, Longman

Figure 4.2

Activity type	Rationale	Description
Choral and individual repetition	To practise rhythm, reduced vowels, stress. To fix pattern in students' minds.	'He was asked to call at the station'. Teacher gets students to repeat and identify reduced vowels and stress.
Drill	Fixing patterns in students' minds, practising forms, illustrating simple question and answer exchange.	Teacher establishes situation. Students are friends of Ted and want to ask about his experience. Teacher has prompts on cards e.g. A: worry / this week ? B: 😊 Teacher indicates student 1 and student 2. Teacher holds up appropriate card. Student 1 looks at card A and says 'Have you been worried this week?' Student 2 looks at B and says 'Yes, I have'. A: ask / station ? B: 😊 Student 1: 'Were you asked to call at the station?' etc. Student 2: 'Yes, I was.'
Structured role play or discourse chain*	Gives slightly more freedom but still practises structure. Could be open or controlled.	You are Ted Robinson. You go to the police. You want to know what happened to your bike. Ask questions beginning When . . . Where . . . What . . . Who . . . You are a policeman. Ted Robinson is asking questions about his bike. Use this information to answer him:

		Found: 10.00 am, Friday 2 April Place: Small village 400 miles away Finder: Farmer in field
Information gap	Allows freer use of language. Injects element of fun and challenge. Control possible if teacher decides who should speak.	Teacher shows picture of Ted's bike 20 years ago to one half of class and picture of Ted's bike when it was found to other. Students ask questions to discover differences and then state: 'The seat was damaged', 'The bell was removed' etc.
Dialogue building	Transfer of language to a different context	Teacher sets scene for students: you arrive home to find your house burgled and vandalised. You telephone the police. Teacher elicits and builds up conversation. A: My house was burgled last night. B: What was taken? A: My bracelet and my purse. B: Was anything damaged? etc.
Personalisation*	Chance to talk freely and find out about one another by completing a questionnaire.	Students asked to find out who has been robbed, who knows someone who was robbed; what was stolen, was it found, was it damaged etc.
Parallel writing	Written consolidation of the passive.	Teacher writes short report on incident that has been investigated. Class builds up similar but different incident. Students write reports using teacher's report as a model.

*Discourse chain Students are given the outline of a dialogue in functional terms e.g. greet, apologise etc. They have to find the words that match the function and build up a dialogue using the clues (see Revell 1979).
*Personalisation Activity which draws significantly on the students' own experience.

Clearly it would be neither wise nor interesting to use all these activities with one class, however they serve to illustrate how variety and interest can be injected while maintaining different degrees of control. Similar techniques can also be used on standard textbook dialogues.

In some contexts supplementary material may not be available and a narrative text may have to be used as the basis of a programme which aims to develop reading as a communicative skill. A useful source of ideas can be found in Williams 1984.

4.5 Improving dialogues

Task

Look at these two extracts. One is a dialogue from an EFL textbook. The other is a transcript of natural speech. Which is which? How can you tell?

1 A: Let's go to the folk club tonight.
   B: No, thanks. I want to watch television. Look, it's Carol's cooking programme.
   A: But we always watch television.
   B: That's not true. Sometimes we listen to records.
   A: All right. But we never go out. Every evening we sit in your flat and do nothing.

2 A: I watched that film last night, remember that – did you see it?
   B: No I'm afraid I didn't – haven't got a television, what was . . .
   A: It's eh, it was about eh, the assassination of President Carter, I think it was.
   A: mm

Commentary

Natural speech tends to be characterised by:
- false starts e.g. It's eh, it was about eh
- incomplete sentences e.g. haven't got a television
- general non specific words and phrases e.g. I think, that's right
- fillers and hesitation devices e.g. well, oh, uhuh, mmm etc.

As such sample 2 is very different from the EFL dialogue in sample 1. This was taken from a recent beginner's book and is a lot closer to natural speech than earlier efforts which were highly stylised and artificial, e.g.

A: I like summer. In summer my father takes us to the beach. I can swim very fast.
B: I like winter.
A: Can you ski?
B: Yes, I can.
A: Can Jane ski, too?   etc.

Communicative language teaching emphasises the importance of exposing students to samples of 'real' language so that they learn to deal with English as it is spoken outside the classroom. Fortunately a lot of recent material has been designed to meet this need, but if you have no alternative to a textbook which is full of unnatural dialogues like the one in the example, the following ideas may help:

Make your own recordings

One simple but effective device might be to make your own recording which is based on the original but would include fillers, hesitation devices and weak forms, (see Rixon 1986).

Cut down on what you use in class

If the objective is to present a structure for the first time, it is actually distracting for students to have to listen to a long dialogue. Assess the dialogue in the book and decide whether it illustrates a natural use of the structure in question. If it does then select part of it for use, after you have built up the context. Try and build in devices like 'Oh really!' and work on developing a natural rhythm and intonation.

Further reading on the importance of listening to natural language can be found in Rixon 1986. An account of teaching conversation is available in Nolasco and Arthur 1987.

4.6 Some principles for materials adaptation

A lot of traditional textbook material can be made more communicative by a number of simple but powerful procedures.

Create an information gap

One of the simplest ways of creating an information gap during pair work is for one of the students to cover up part of, or shut, the textbook. This means that one of the students has access to information the other student does not have and there is a reason for asking and answering questions.

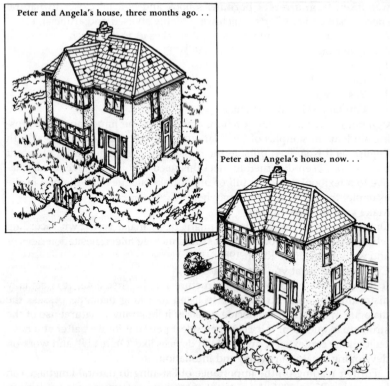

Figure 4.3

Old Task: Ask for or supply information about what Peter and Angela have done, like this:

Have they mended the roof yet?

Yes they have.

New task: Work in two teams. Team A should cover up the picture of Peter and Angela's house as it is today. Team B should cover up the picture of the house as it was three months ago. The members of both teams are friends of Peter and Angela. Team B visited the house yesterday. Team A visited three months ago and should find out about the changes by asking questions like:

Have they mended the roof yet? etc

When you finish check your answers by looking at the textbook again. (The same task can be done in pairs.)

---

48 Family life

LEVEL	**Intermediate and above**
TIME	**25–30 minutes**
AIM	To get students to share opinions.
PREPARATION	Prepare a task sheet along the following lines, and make photocopies for your class.

TASK SHEET	Work in groups of three or four. Decide which of the following statements you agree with and which statements you disagree with. Discuss these with the other members of your group. Try to modify any statements you disagree with so that they represent the opinions of your group. Be ready to report your discussion to the teacher.

1 Children should only leave home after they are married.
2 Old people should be encouraged to stay in old people's homes rather than with the family.
3 People should not have more than two children.
4 Children should always obey their parents.
5 You should always ask your parents for permission to marry.
6 Children should pay their parents rent when they get a job.
7 You should always be ready to help a member of the family.
8 The members of a family should live in the same area so that it is easy for them to visit each other.
9 Family life is less important in the modern world than it was in the past.

From *Resource Books for Teachers – Conversation* by Nolasco & Arthur, Oxford University Press

Figure 4.4

This task is an example of a communicative activity which encourages personalisation. Personalisation involves encouraging students to make contributions from their own knowledge, experience and view of the world and it is a powerful way of encouraging them to communicate.

Tasks such as the one above can be difficult to handle in a large class, with students who are not used to working independently, but the principle can be applied to any material by the use of the following techniques.

- Getting students to relate to the topic by eliciting their knowledge of the topic in the warm-up phase. So students about to study the topic illustrated above could be asked questions as follows:

    Have you ever moved house?

    Did you move to a new house?

    Was there a lot to do?

    What did you change?   etc.

- Getting students to provide prompts e.g. a task like 'Write down five things you need to fix in your house' could be used to generate the prompts for practice about Peter and Angela's house.

- Getting students to use the language presented in a context related to their own experience.

    This is extremely difficult as successful personalisation goes beyond asking students to use a particular model to talk about themselves, i.e. it is more than changing 'Aunt Agatha likes oranges' to 'I like apples'. Personalisation should include an element of genuine information exchange which we need to motivate by devising special tasks. For example, it is possible to extend course book material by systematically exploiting interest in other people.

What day is today?
It is **Monday**.

Miss Kato:	What day is today, Kumi?
Kumi:	It is Saturday.
Miss Kato:	What is the date today, Ken?
Ken:	It is November 7. Today is Kumi's birthday.
Miss Kato:	Happy birthday, Kumi!
Kumi:	Thank you.

From *Hew Horizons in English I* by Mellgren and Walker, Addison-Wesley

Figure 4.5

Additional task

Ask students to listen to the teacher and the other members of the class and complete a class birthday chart.

Jan	Feb	Mar	April	May	June	July	Aug	Sept	Oct	Nov	Dec
Alexis 3rd	Lena 14th		Max 5th		Michelle 2nd		Jean 10th	Sarah 6th	Ralph 15th		Lisa 18th
			Paul 12th		Anna 22nd			David 19th			Sam 21st

Figure 4.6 A birthday chart

In this example, the source of the idea is a more recent school textbook which includes communicative language teaching activities, (Vincent, Foll and Cripwell 1985). As we mentioned earlier it is very important to be on the lookout for ideas which you can use.

- Relate practice material to the student's own experience. It is always worth considering the extent to which we can make practice material more meaningful by relating it to the student's own experience e.g. this is an example of a predictive dialogue where a certain choice by A will prescribe corresponding choices by B:

    A: Do you like X?
    B: Yes, I love it, thank you.
    A: Do you prefer Y?

X coffee	Y black or white
roast duck	breast or leg
wine	red or white

(The choices have been put in the right order)

Students who were familiar with certain aspects of western culture would have little trouble with the exercise, but many students would enjoy the challenge of devising their own choices so we might get alternative items such as green or brown lentils in the Middle East and omelette or seaweed 'sushi' in Japan. The choices can be built up on the board through a process of discussion with the class as a whole, an approach which sets up genuine teacher/class communication. When the complete exercise has been put up on the board the students can move on to practise the dialogue in pairs.

Make use of the student's imagination
Texts, visuals and even sound material can all be a stimulus for tasks in which students go beyond what is provided by responding to questions like:

Figure 4.7
From *Poem into Poem*,
by A Maley and S Moulding,
CUP

How would you feel if you were the man/woman?
What do you think he/she might be saying?
When do you think the photograph was taken?
Where are the men going?   etc.
Although this photograph was chosen to promote discussion, many text-book illustrations and texts can be exploited in a similar way.

Make use of the student's personal resources
Students love a challenge. Getting them to use their own resources for learning is one way of exploiting this. Ask them to cut an 'action' photo-graph (e.g. a sports scene, a scene from a film) from a newspaper or magazine and bring it to class. A traditional way to approach it would be to do question and answer work such as: What is he doing? He is . . .
A more communicative version would be to ask students to look at the picture in order to try to remember as much detail of the actions as

possible. Ideas are elicited and written on the board (even if they are factually incorrect). When students have finished they can then be asked to look at the picture again and check the sentences on the board. If necessary they should reformulate their sentences. This is similar to a well-known activity called 'Kim's Game' (see Rixon 1981). Many other children's games can be adapted for classroom use.

4.7 Adapting communicative techniques

The interest in teaching English as communication means that there are now several interesting and useful handbooks which contain examples of communicative activities. Some of these activities include:
- mingling activities
- ranking activities
- values clarification activities
- problem solving tasks
- mini projects

A ranking task

NASA game

Aims	*Skills* – speaking
	Language – giving and asking for reasons, expressing certainty and uncertainty, making objections
	Other – general knowledge
Level	Intermediate/advanced
Organisation	Individuals, pairs
Preparation	Handout (see Part 2)
Time	10–15 minutes
Procedure	*Step 1:* Each student is given the handout and asked to rank the 15 items. (Note that the moon has no atmosphere, so it is impossible to make fire or to transmit sound signals; the moon has no magnetic poles.)
	Step 2: Each student then compares his solution with that of his neighbour and they try to arrive at a common ranking.
	Step 3: The results of Step 2 are discussed and compared around the class.
Remarks	(Idea adapted from Rogers 1978.)

You are one of the crew on board a spaceship to rendezvous with the mother ship on the lighted side of the moon. Mechanical difficulties, however, have forced your ship to crashland at a spot some 300 kilometres from the rendezvous point. The rough landing has damaged much of the equipment aboard. Your survival depends on reaching the mother ship, and you have to choose the most essential items for the 300 km. trip. The 15 items left intact after landing are listed below. Your task is to rank them in order of their importance to your crew in your attempt to reach the rendezvous point. Write number 1 for the most important item, number 2 for the second most important item, and so on through to number 15.

box of matches	star map
concentrated food	life raft
20 metres of nylon rope	magnetic compass
parachute silk	20 litres of water
portable heating unit	signal flares
two .45 calibre pistols	first-aid kit
one case of tins of dried milk	solar-powered FM receiver/
two 50 kilo tanks of oxygen	transmitter

From *Keep Talking* by F. Klippel, Cambridge University Press

A values task

A dream society?

Task 1

Work in groups of five or six students.

Imagine that you have all gone to live on a 'dream island'. On this island you have everything you need to live quite well, food, water, housing, roads, transport, etc. All you need to do is decide how you are going to live peacefully together.

Look at the following statements. They could be the rules of your dream society.

- Nobody is allowed to own property.
- Everyone has total freedom to do whatever he/she wants.
- 'Love your neighbour.'
- Everyone will have the chance to do what he/she is interested in to help the group.
- The group will meet once a month to discuss problems.
- The group will have a leader elected by the others.
- Everyone in the group will be allowed to travel from the island whenever he/she wants.
- Nothing will be brought to the island without the agreement of the others.
- There will be a programme of sport, music and other entertainment for everyone.
- Women may have children but marriage to one partner is not allowed.

Do you agree with them?

Change any that you disagree with and add others if you wish.

Put the final list of rules in order of importance for keeping peace in the society. (The most important should be number 1 and so on.)

From *Speaking: Elementary* by Rob Nolasco, Oxford University Press.

A mini project

Pollution affects many things: buildings, rivers, animals, the air which we breathe, the sea.

1 Find out about how pollution is affecting your town or your country.

2 Make a poster about the problem.

From *Project English* by T. Hutchinson, Oxford University Press

Although some of these ideas originated in school classrooms they may need adapting for your particular classes. The following questions are especially relevant in assessing the suitability of such material.

1 What are the management risks involved?
   Are the students used to this type of activity? Will they know what to do? Are there likely to be discipline problems arising from long periods of unsupervised group work, students moving around the room etc? Is the activity workable in its present form or does it require too much furniture moving etc?

2 Is the task culturally acceptable?
   Does it conform to student expectations? Will they see it as an appropriate learning activity? Is any aspect of the task or the linguistic and non-linguistic data likely to be offensive?

3 Does the task pose an appropriate linguistic challenge?
   Is the task too easy or too difficult? Will the students understand the instructions? Do they have the linguistic resources to complete the task?

4 Does the task pose an appropriate cognitive challenge?
   Is the task too trivial or too difficult? Does it ask for too much creativity?

5 Does the task require outside material such as dictionaries etc? Is such material available?

Obviously only you can answer these questions. However, it is possible to overcome many of these implied problems in the following ways.

Prepare students for the task
A lot of the management risks disappear if we prepare students for the task. Preparation might include showing learners exactly what is expected of them when they are doing a specific type of task.

Task

In ranking activities students are required to put the items from a given list into an order of importance or preference. This rearranging phase is usually followed by a period of discussion when students explain or defend their choice. Look at this task from *English teaching forum* for October 1984.

MEMBERS OF WHICH PROFESSION MAKE THE BEST HUSBANDS?

In small groups, discuss and rank the following professions according to which ones produce the best husbands, giving reasons for the choices and trying to reach a consensus. Then put each group's list on the blackboard and compare. Men should think of this question from their (future?) wives' point of view: Which profession would my wife most or least like me to be in?

football player	dress designer	night watchman
king	pop singer	movie star
bullfighter	skier	salesman
fireman	English teacher	sailor

What problems would you expect if you gave this task to an intermediate class who have not encountered a ranking activity before? How might you adapt the task? How would you prepare the students for such a task?

Commentary

Obviously it would depend on the group but one would expect that most students who had not done this form of activity before would get little out of the task if it were presented to them in its present form. Clearly you would think about making the instructions clearer. In some cultures one might also want to change some of the professions. The most important thing is to think through preparing the students rather than throwing them straight into a group task. A possible sequence is as follows.

1 Set out the objectives of the task through oral discussion.
2 Elicit criteria for good and bad husbands. Supply whatever vocabulary they might need and put it up on the board.
3 Students rank the professions individually.

4   Ask a few of the better students to give reasons for their choice along the lines of 'A nightwatchman is the best because he is at home during the day' etc.
5   Tell students to work in small groups and see if they can agree on one list.
6   Ask members of the group to report to the class.

Some classes might not be ready for the small group work at stage 5 and pair work is an alternative. Similar procedures can be used with other types of activities. As students get used to such activities it will become increasingly easy to move straight into group work.

Make the task more accessible
Other ways of making a task more accessible:
- Give students extra time to complete a task. If a task is unfamiliar to students they may need more time to work out the procedure to follow.
- Help students with the instructions.
- Give them a pre-task to introduce them to the language and/or the cultural concepts they will need.
- Retain the elements of the task while changing the cultural content to suit the age, interests and needs of your students.

4.8   Games and competitions

In addition to the personal challenge, younger students also enjoy competing with their peers, and introducing a game element is a way of livening up any material. There are useful collections of games and it is possible to orientate them to material the students must learn, (see Rixon 1981, Carrier and The CBT 1980 and Wright et al 1979). However, many games (including some of the examples here!) are highly controlled. Controlled games are useful as pre-communicative activities (see Littlewood 1981). They provide plenty of opportunities for practice, they involve students and they prepare them for freer work because they are less formal than many traditional language learning activities. However, they should not be viewed as a substitute for the genuinely communicative games which are the ultimate aim.

Task
Look at these examples of games. Which ones are most controlled? Why? Which ones are least controlled? Why?.

FOOTBALL (A revision game)

Level   Beginner, intermediate
Aim   To revise any material
Materials A small paper circle (the ball), some Blu tak* or a coin
             if using an OHP
Preparation A set of questions

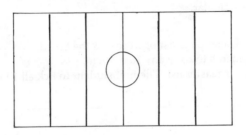

Procedure

1 Draw a pitch on the blackboard or OHP and place the ball in
   the centre circle.
2 Divide the class into two teams.
3 Toss a coin to see which team will answer the first question.
   Members of each team answer questions in order. If the answer
   is right advance the ball one line towards the opponents' goal.
   If the answer is wrong offer it to any member of the other
   team. If there is too much noise, cheating etc., offer a penalty
   to the other side. This has a magic effect! Goals are scored
   when a team reaches the goal line.

Comments

We have used this game very successfully with adolescents who enjoy the
competition. It is possible to keep order if the referee is strict. Questions
can be on any aspect of language, e.g. spell X, and centred around work
students have been doing. Grade the questions so that weaker students
get questions they can answer. It is usually possible to make sure the
result is a close one.

*Trade name for a reusable adhesive which is very useful for putting visuals on a
blackboard.

WORD BINGO

Level	Beginner, low, intermediate
Aim	Revision of vocabulary and pronunciation
Preparation	Choose a list of about 20 words from the coursebook. Aim for items which contain phonological problems e.g. 13 and 30. Write a shorter master list which contains 15 items. Avoid having two items which are similar.

Procedure

1 Write the complete list of words on the board.
2 Ask students to copy any 10 of them.
3 Read your master list. The first student to tick all 10 words wins.

Comments

This game is a fun way of revising words. A variant is to draw 10 to 15 stick pictures on the board. Tell students to copy any 5. Read a random list of the names of the objects.

THE LEGO GAME

Level	Intermediate to advanced
Aim	To practise oral/aural skills
Preparation	Collect together LEGO sets or similar children's building materials and step by step diagrams showing how to build various models. Ideally there should be a set of builing materials and instructions for each pair.

Procedure

1 Divide the class into pairs (A and B).
2 Explain that player A will get the instructions for how to build a LEGO model. He must not show it to player B. Player B has the pieces necessary to build the model. Player A describes how the model should be put together. Player B may ask questions if he wishes.
3 Monitor the activity.
4 Ask B to compare his completed model with the diagram.

From *How to Use Games in Language Teaching* by S Rixon, Macmillan

The third activity is the least controlled, and centred entirely on free communication. Unlike the other games in this section there is no constraint on what the students might say in order to be successful. Obviously, in many classes students will need to be prepared to take part in such an open activity (see Chapter 3) and the activity itself may need adapting for use in a large class – it would be very difficult to assemble enough building materials for 20 pairs – but it is possible to get students to give each other instructions in how to make a paper model. Controlled games are a good way of making lessons more lively while preparing students for games which centre entirely on communication, but it is a mistake to equate the use of games with communicative language teaching.

4.9 Summary

The first step in teaching more communicatively is to look at the activities you use in your classrooms to see the sort of interaction they generate. If the textbook you use does not allow students a chance to determine what they want to say, present a challenge etc, you can think about adapting or supplementing it. A lot of 'traditional' material can be made more communicative by changing the activities based on these materials and it is also possible to adapt materials which have been designed for use in small classes to the large class situation.

4.10 Consolidation tasks

1 Look at this dialogue from *Streamline English Departures* published by Oxford University Press.

Mr Dean:	Good evening.
Receptionist:	Good evening, sir.
	What's your name, please?
Mr Dean:	My name's Dean.
Receptionist:	Ah, yes . . . Mr Dean . . . Room 15. Here's your key.
Mr Dean:	Thank you.
Porter:	Is this your case?
Mr Dean:	No, it isn't.
Porter:	Oh, is that your case over there?
Mr Dean:	Yes, it is.

Discuss different techniques for exploiting the language in this dialogue communicatively.

2 Collect at least one example of the following types of communicative task.

A values clarification task

A ranking activity

A questionnaire activity

An information gap activity which does not use visuals.

Which activity do you think would be the easiest to introduce? Why? Which activity do you think would be the most difficult to introduce? Why? Decide on the modifications you would need to make the activity work in your classroom.

3 Choose a short section of the textbook you are using in class e.g. one unit. Now try and use the ideas on pages 61 to 68 of this book to make your coursebook more communicative.

If possible discuss your conclusions with a colleague.

4.11 Further reading

Useful sources of communicative activities can be found in the bibliography. Klippel 1984 contains particularly useful introductions to some of the types of communicative activities. Articles on materials adaptation sometimes appear in *English Language Teaching Journal*, *Practical English Teaching* and *Modern English Teacher*. A typology of communicative exercises developed by a German secondary group has been edited and translated into English by C Candlin (Candlin 1981).

5 Coping with limited resources

Teachers of large classes often have to cope with limited resources such as a shortage of suitable textbooks and other print materials, in addition to the physical problems of having large numbers of students in classrooms with rows of heavy desks which are impossible to move. Many of these problems can be overcome and any classroom can be made more communicative using the resources which are normally available in any country.

5.1 Organising the classroom

Organising a room to suit the activity can influence the interaction and the success of the activity enormously. For pair and group work we need an arrangement which makes it easy for the participants to communicate with each other and for the teacher to see and be seen. During the presentation of new language the teacher is the focal point of attention and students must be able to see the teacher, the board and any visual aids clearly. So, there is rarely an optimum layout and ideally we should aim at altering the seating in the classroom in order to suit particular tasks.

Task 1
Look at the following illustrations and decide which of the arrangements would be most suitable for the Activities A to H described on pages 51 to 53 in Chapter 3.

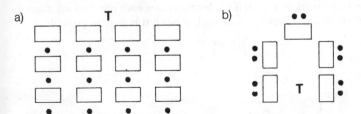

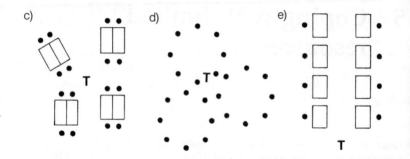

Figure 5.1

While arrangements such as c) and d) serve to facilitate communication independently of the teacher and would therefore be most suitable for Activities E, F and H it is often impossible to group desks in this way in the average large class because of the nature of the furniture and the need to share the classroom with teachers who may have other requirements. Even where the ideal is impossible we should always consider the extent to which we can arrange the seating so that opportunities for student to student communication can be maximised. For example, an arrangement such as the one below makes it easier for the students to see each other and this is a considerable advantage during drills and open pair work.

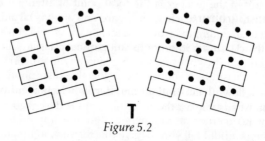

Figure 5.2

In closed pair work it is ideal if students can see each other so ask them to move their chairs in order to face each other if this is at all possible.

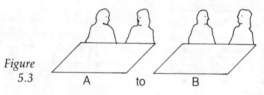

Figure 5.3

If it is important that students do not see what their partner is doing they can be asked to work back to back or to create a simple barrier with a textbook or bag.

In cases where it is impossible to move the chairs at all because they are fixed to the desks, communication can be facilitated by asking students to turn round to face the person behind them. This may be the best option in a situation where the desks are in single rows.

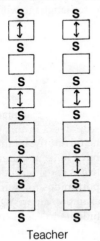

Figure 5.4
Ask students to turn round

5.2 Moving furniture

If you decide to change the normal seating of the class it is important that you think through the changes before giving any instructions to start, as moving furniture can be a source of considerable disruption. If necessary move one section of the class at a time. It may help to identify sections of the class e.g. row 1 or group A.

The following instructions will help to minimise any problems.

1 Do not move until I tell you to (give this instruction first to ensure that students will pay attention to everything you have to say).

2 Lift your chair (and desk) quietly! (this helps to minimise the amount of noise from scraping furniture).

If you share the classroom you should leave enough time for the students to move the furniture back before the bell rings for the end of the lesson. Remember that moving about the classroom is a habit and as soon as students get used to the procedure the noise and chaos will soon be reduced to a minimum.

5.3 Using the board

Many school classrooms will have a blackboard rather than the whiteboard which is becoming fashionable in some teaching situations. The general uses of the board can be summarised as follows:
- to present information for students to copy and learn
- to give instructions for tasks, homework etc.
- to present visuals and other material as a basis for language work
- to build up a lesson summary.

There are a variety of boards available.

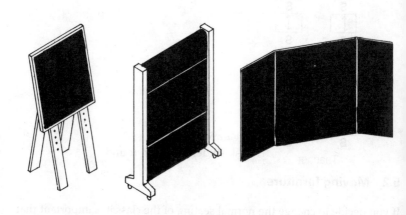

Figure 5.5   Easel board   Roll-over board   Flapped board

A board which is fixed directly to the wall is the most common but the advantage of the boards which are illustrated is that they are particularly suited to creating an information gap by concealing information from the students e.g. by fixing a visual behind a flap or on the other side of an easel blackboard. A similar effect can be achieved with a traditional blackboard through the use of a large sheet to cover up a section of the blackboard. These techniques can help to introduce a game element and increase student participation. The board is a very flexible teaching aid and the aim of this section is to give some practical examples which we hope will be a stimulus to further development. See Morgan Bowen 1982 (48–56) for further ideas, although some may need to be adapted for use in a large class.

5.4 Using the blackboard to save duplication

Some books and articles assume that all teachers have unlimited copying facilities and can afford the time and materials to make numerous handouts. Try using the blackboard instead. You will find it is often more effective than another piece of paper. Here are some ideas:

1 Write a text, e.g. a letter, on the central part of the board and obscure part of the text, e.g. by closing one flap. Students have to reconstruct the text using prediction skills.

2 Write a short text on the board with the sentences in the wrong order. Students read and re-write the text in the correct order. This emphasises the importance of devices which join text together.

3 Write a text or a dialogue on the board. Erase a few words and ask students to reconstruct the original orally. Progressively erase more and more of the text and dialogue so that students need to hold more of the original in their memory.

4 Present additional practice material. In many large classes some of the students will finish coursebook activities well in advance of others. Training them to look to the blackboard for additional material is a useful way of coping with what can otherwise be a discipline problem.

5.5 Words on the board

Many teachers seem to have time to make a lot of aids, but what is practicable with 12 students is often impossible with 40 or more. Instead of spending time cutting up slips of paper and then distributing them in class, use the blackboard as a focal point for the activity.

FOCUS ON THE BOARD	
Aim	Focus on text structure
Level	Any
Preparation	Write a short text on pieces of paper, i.e. cut up into words and phrases. Put Blu-tak (or similar) on the back.
Procedure	Students come out one at a time and build up text by selecting an appropriate word or phrase and sticking it up.

Doing this with an entire letter is one way of introducing learners to the way letters are laid out. At the start the board might look something like this.

Figure 5.6

As you can see the board is an excellent medium for presenting input which can be a stimulus for language learning.

5.6 The board as a focal point for output

The board can also be used to elicit creative language use. Some ideas include:

1 Get students to come up and contribute to a group story. Start the story with a sentence e.g. 'It was late one night . . .' and offer the chalk to one of the students who completes the sentence in any way he chooses. When the student finishes the chalk is offered to another student and so on. Do not interfere except to keep order. The students should be responsible for corrections, introducing joining words etc.

2 Draw an image on the board to set the scene.

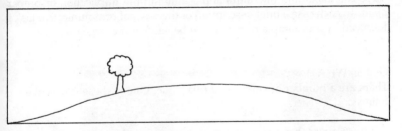

Figure 5.7

Get students to translate what they see into words. Accept any suggestions, add additional elements and invite more suggestions.

Figure 5.8

Get students to build up the story until it reaches a conclusion. Ask students to retell the story or write it down.

5.7 Using communicative activities without much duplication

All the activities in this section rely on an information gap in which one of the participants has information which the others do not have. They are used frequently in communicative classrooms and can also be used in large classes if:

- students are used to working independently of the teacher
- you are able to produce enough visual aids
- you can distribute and collect the material quickly and efficiently.

It would be more communicative to carry out all of these activities in pairs but many teachers find it impossible to assemble enough visuals. It is, however, possible to adapt these activities for use in the large class so that there is a maximum of control and a minimum of duplication or preparation. In each case a brief description of the original communicative task is followed by an example of how it can be used in the large class.

GUESS WHAT!

There are a number of versions of this game. One of these is described as follows:

> One player takes a card and the others must ask him questions to find out what is on it. He is only allowed to answer yes or no. The person who guesses correctly keeps the card and the winner is the one with the most cards at the end of the game. The pack of cards may consist of objects, famous living people or famous people of the past.
>
> (Morgan Bowen 1982)

Aim   Practice in yes/no questions
Level   Any
Procedure
1   Fix a picture to the board so that students cannot see it, (a flapped blackboard is ideal), or hold it so that only you can see it.
2   Allow the students to ask you (or a student who has seen the picture) questions which will help them to determine what is in the picture. Limit them to yes/no questions such as 'Is it big?', 'Is it made of wood?' etc. It is possible to make the activity more challenging by limiting the number of questions the students can ask and/or increasing the detail on the picture.

ASK AND DRAW

'Describe and draw' is a well-known communicative game. It is described as follows:

> Student A has a picture. He describes it to student B who cannot see it. Student B attempts to draw the picture according to Student A's description. Student A may watch what B is doing and offer advice and correction where necessary. Student B can question student A and ask

for more information if he wishes. Finally the students compare their versions.

(Morgan Bowen 1982)

This activity can also be used in the large class if you have a stock of pictures etc. This version which offers greater control can be used to introduce students to the idea.

Aim   Practice in comparisons, spatial relationships and questions
Level   Elementary and above
Procedure
1   Make a drawing of a number of objects and hide it from the students
2   Explain that you have a drawing of (name the objects) and tell them that they have to ask questions so that they can draw exactly the same picture in their notebooks. Elicit a few examples such as: 'Is the . . . to the left of the . . .?', 'Is the . . . bigger than the . . .?'
3   Show the students your picture and elicit the differences between their pictures and yours.

Figure 5.9

SPOT THE DIFFERENCE – with a difference
'Spot the difference' is a common information gap type activity. It can be described as follows:

> Each player has a picture. The two pictures are identical except for a specified number of small differences. The players are not allowed to show each other their pictures, but through discussion they must identify the differences. The discussion may take the form of talking about their own pictures or asking the other player questions about his picture.

(Morgan Bowen 1982)

Figure 5.10

Aim	To carry out 'spot the difference' in a large class with a minimum of duplication
Level	Any
Preparation	Make a version of visuals which are big enough for the class to see, (see page 96 for guidance)
Procedure	The following alternatives are possible:

1 Display one of the pictures and hide the other so that only you can see it. Tell students to ask questions to work out the difference between the picture they can see and the one you have hidden.

2 Divide the class into two so that one half can see one picture and the other half the other. One way this can be done is as follows. Ask students to discover the differences by asking questions. Setting up the classroom in this way allows you to nominate, if you prefer to, who should ask and answer the questions.

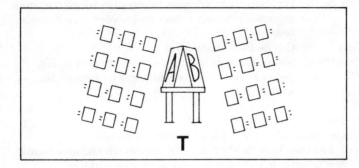

Figure 5.11

3 Arrange the students so that they sit in pairs but facing
  opposite directions so that they can only see one of the visuals
  each. They then carry out the same activity in pairs.

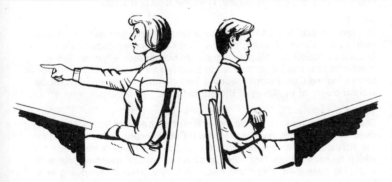

Figure 5.12

JIGSAW PIECES

'Jigsaw' texts (either listening or reading) is where individual students
or groups of students are given slightly different texts concerning a
single event so that they have to exchange information with each other
before some final task can be completed.

(Gower and Walters 1983)

Aim	For students to interpret information which they must share with the other students in order to complete a task.
Level	Can be used at any level
Preparation	Simple texts (so that they are easy to read from a distance) and a task (see example for intermediate students)

Procedure
1 Put the texts on opposite walls.
2 Give students a few minutes to process the text.
3 When they have finished take the texts down and give them a few minutes to complete the task with their partner.

A jigsaw task
Make notes of the important information in the text you can see. Share your information with your partner and write one text which contains information from both originals. Give the new text a title.

Text 1
The term 'robot' first came into the language through literature. It was used by the Czech playwright Karel Capek in his play *Rossums's Universal Robots*. In this play robots are humanoids – human-like machines that can be factory-made quickly and cheaply. The word robot comes from a Czech word meaning forced work, or slavery. So, robots were thought of as slaves of the human race.

Text 2
Seventy years ago no one had ever heard of the word 'robot'. It was first used by a Czechslovakian writer, Karel Capek (pronounced Chapek) in the 1920s. He wrote a play about a scientist who invents machines which he calls robots, from the Czech word 'robota' meaning 'slave-like' work. He gave them this name because they were used for doing very boring work. At the end of the play the robots kill their human owners and take over the world.

Figure 5.13

5.8 Beyond print – ideas for creative language use

A communicative classroom should aim to involve students in creative language use. The following types of activities allow for this while saving paper and duplication.

1 Recording a sequence of sounds (with optional dialogue) is a good way of eliciting a narrative composition which is 'original' in the sense that the outcome will depend on the way in which students interpret the stimulus material.

> **Sound effects script**
>
> alarm clock
> yawn
> running water
> banging and knocking sound at door
> footsteps running down stairs
> door opening
> short scream/thud
> door closing
> gentle music

2 Providing material which aims to stimulate students to be creative through the use of techniques which need nothing more than a blackboard or a collection of realia that can be collected anywhere. These may include:
  - A collection of images or objects which must be included in a story. These may suggest a theme but they will not determine the storyline.

Figure 5.14   Write a 100-word story in which each of the objects appears at least once

  - Creating a situation which students have to interpret. For example, students could be asked to describe a person from objects 'found' in their pockets or dustbin.

In each case these activities should be done either individually or in pairs before a session in which students have to read their versions to the other students. Although students have to be very creative these activities are reassuring in that they are carried out in a very traditional framework.

5.9 Student notebooks

When resources are limited a student's notebook becomes a vital learning tool. Each teaching situation will require different amounts of written work but the notebook should be viewed and developed as a personal learning tool. Some of the uses to which a notebook can be put include:

- A personal record of the focal point of grammar lessons. Students should be encouraged to enter these in a form that is clear and easy to follow. (Useful sources of information for the teacher include *Ways to Grammar, Basic English Usage* and *Practical English Usage*.)

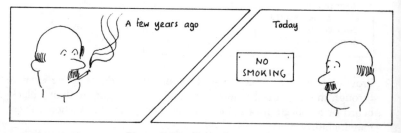

Figure 5.15   'I used to smoke'

- A personal record of vocabulary.

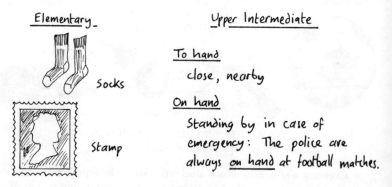

Figure 5.16

- A section for poems, songs, puzzles, games etc.

Obviously, exactly what is included will depend on the age, interests and needs of the students but showing them sample pages and discussing what might be included is a form of learner training that should not be neglected. Encourage students to have pride in their notebooks and check their organisation and presentation regularly on a random basis. Give praise/award stars for good record books, and if a photocopier is available make a copy for the class noticeboard (see page 97).

5.10 Making material go further

In many situations duplicating facilities are limited and expensive so teachers have to find ways to make material go further. Ways of saving paper (and effort) include:

- Separate texts and the activities related to them. It is possible to save paper by putting the questions on the board. The same text can also be used for different purposes and possibly at different levels.
- Number the handouts issued to students so that they can be collected back efficiently. In many cases, e.g. visuals, it is not necessary for students to keep material. In other cases it may be worth training students to extract important information for themselves (see the section on notebooks).
- Sharing of texts and exercise sheets. This encourages students to work together and collaborate, and can be promoted as a virtue rather than a necessity.

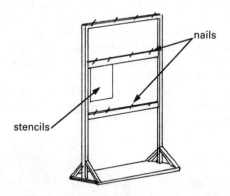

Figure 5.17   Stencil storage frame

In many countries stencils remain the most common method of reproducing print material cheaply. If these are stored correctly they can be re-used provided care is taken of them. One fairly practical method of storing stencils is to have a simple wooden frame made. It is then possible to hang large numbers of stencils from the nails. The best way to preserve them is to dry them as they come off the machine by placing a piece of absorbent paper on the wet surface, as this will soak up the excess ink and stop the stencil from developing unwanted creases. Write a large number (and the title) at the top of each stencil and enter the same number on a duplicated copy to be held in a master file (a ring binder is particularly suitable). This will make it relatively easy for you to find the correct stencil after a period of time, as well as allow for materials sharing. Whatever storage system you decide on, make sure the material is catalogued and filed. This will save a lot of time and effort as it is often possible to adapt existing materials for re-use elsewhere.

5.11 Making wall pictures

Large sheets of art paper can be very expensive so it is worth looking out for substitutes. Plain wallpaper, and the paper used to wrap-up the dry-cleaning in some countries, work extremely well. Sketch out your design in pencil before resorting to the broad felt-tipped markers which are ideal for the strong lines needed to ensure that the illustrations are clearly visible to everyone. Keep them simple.

The easiest way to enlarge pictures is to use an epidiascope. If you happen to have one available all you need do is place the picture you want to enlarge in the machine. An image of the drawing can then be projected onto the paper, which you have stuck on the wall, and the lines drawn in with a broad felt-tipped pen. However, these machines are not often found outside teacher's colleges or resource centres! It is also possible to use an OHP to similar effect. Trace the drawing with an OHP pen onto a transparency, project the image onto a piece of paper which is stuck on the wall and draw the lines with a broad felt-tipped pen. It is also possible to use a pantograph.

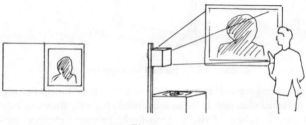

Figure 5.18

If none of the above are available a more time-consuming method is to scale up. Draw one centimetre squares in pencil over the picture to be enlarged. Then draw the same number of squares on the paper you want to use making the squares five or ten times larger. Use the squares as a guideline for copying the original.

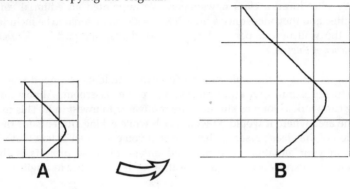

Figure 5.19

5.12 The living wall

One way of making any classroom more communicative is to have a class noticeboard (and this may be little more than a large sheet of paper) or an area of the wall on which students are encouraged to make contributions. Different things will work with different classes but here are some of the things teachers have told us about.

'I introduced a "puzzle corner" in which I put simple puzzles in English which I cut out from newspapers and magazines. After one or two weeks I encouraged students to contribute their own puzzles in English so that we could decide on a puzzle of the week. This worked very well and there were often students grouped around the board trying to solve the problems and in many cases copying them into their notebook.' (*A British teacher with a class of 14 year olds in Greece.*)

'I encourage my students to write to pen friends from all over the world in English. I have a corner where students can display copies of their letters, photographs they have received etc. Each new addition is always a source of great curiosity and interest.' (*A Spanish secondary teacher.*)

'I introduced an area where I could display excerpts from students' work that I thought would be of interest to the others. I noticed a far higher standard of work immediately.' (*A British teacher in a Moroccan secondary school.*)

'We introduced a class newspaper. We appointed an editorial committee and they meet once a month to decide on material to be included in the wall newspaper. A lot of the students take part.' (*A German teacher of English.*)

Having an area of the wall which will attract students is a good way of introducing extra input and brightening up the classroom. Almost anything can work as long as students are motivated to invest in it. This may be one area where it would be well worth while asking students for their opinion of the ideas presented here, so that you choose an option that will work in your situation. The main advantage of these projects is that students get experience of communicating with each other in English.

5.13 Student-produced materials

Students often enjoy helping in the production of materials. One area for student involvement is the making of flash cards and similar items to build up the supply of visual aids. Many students will have access to old magazines, glue etc and these can easily be turned into visuals. Ways in which this can work include:
- asking students to bring any pictures they find interesting to class. They can then select some for mounting.
- asking students to bring pictures related to a particular theme or topic, e.g. students could bring photographs of six things they would like to take on holiday.
- having students make small cards for vocabulary drills etc.

Husband
You've just bought a new suit. It's fantastic. The jacket fits perfectly and the trousers are beautiful. You're very proud of it. Show it to your wife.

> *Wife*
> Your husband is wearing a new suit. It's awful. The jacket's too big, the trousers are too short and the colour's horrible. Get him to take it back to the shop.

> *Husband's Sister*
> Your brother is wearing a new suit. It makes him look a bit fat, but it's a nice colour. Be kind to him, and don't let your sister-in-law be too nasty.

From *Teaching Techniques for Communicative English* by J Revell, Macmillan

Figure 5.20

Students can also write materials! For example, a well-used communicative activity involves the use of role cards. (See Revell 1979, Porter Ladousse 1987.)

We have found it is possible to get advanced students to write very effective role plays for use with classes at a lower level. The procedure is as follows:

1 Give students an example of a role play which is similar to the one above so they can see how it works.
2 Ask students to work in groups and imagine a situation which involves a number of people in a social problem and/or interpersonal conflict. They should sketch out the broad outline of the story before producing role cards for all the participants in the situation.

Here is an outline of an example, which was produced by advanced students in Angola for use with an elementary class.

> *Introduction*
> Ernestina receives a final demand to pay her rates by the end of the day. If she does not she will lose her home. She has no money and therefore has to persuade a taxi driver to take her to her uncle who listens to her story and agrees to help. When she finally arrives at the tax office just before it closes they will not accept the money as she has not brought her identification. She has to try and solve the problem with the help of a clerk.

> ### Ernestina
> You are Ernestina. You must pay your rates by the end of the day etc. You have no money. Ask the taxi driver to take you to your uncle etc.
> Some useful expressions: 'Can you help me . . .?', 'Please take me . . .'

> ### Taxi driver
> You are a taxi driver. A woman asks you for help. Find out about her problem. Offer to help her etc.

This type of activity works very well with the lower level students. It combines control and support with creativity in a situation students can readily identify with. The students who produce the activities also enjoy it and benefit from the fact that they always try very hard to avoid error or inappropriacy.

5.14   Bringing in the outside world

One of the best ways of making any classroom more communicative is to encourage students to correspond in English. This can be done by:

1   Setting up a direct link to a class in Britain or another English speaking country.
2   Through pen-pal clubs.
3   Helping your students contact organisations or individuals.

As English is an international language your students may wish to write to clubs in non English-speaking countries too, indicating that they wish to correspond in English. Individuals who write should always include details of age, sex, school or university (if applicable) and their interests. Make an introductory letter the subject of a writing lesson to give students the confidence they need to start writing.

Approaching organisations on behalf of your students

If you decide to write to an agency or organisation on behalf of your class it is important to give the organisers information about the age, background and level of English of your students. You should also give an idea of the number of students who want to correspond. A list of organisations who can put you in touch with correspondents is on page 128.

Developing the correspondence

If the correspondence develops students may well be interested by further writing lessons which aim to help them describe their family, home town, local festivals etc., in letter form. One way this support can be provided is to give them models in the form of letters 'received' which supply similar information. The model can be discussed before students are asked to rewrite their own version which will usually involve them in substituting factual information.

Other activities for bringing in the outside world

Asking English-speaking visitors who are not teachers to come into a class and give a short talk and respond to questions is another way of stimulating real language use if the right person can be found. Discuss the visit so that the speaker and students know what is expected of them as it can be very demotivating for students to listen to a long talk which they cannot understand. Topics which students may find interesting include:

- an illustrated talk on part of the speaker's native country
- an illustrated talk about a hobby or personal interest.

The main advantage is that a visiting speaker gives students a real reason for listening and asking questions, and as English is an international language the speaker could be a national of any country!

Such visits might be incorporated into a project (see Chapter 6). Ideas for further out of class activities can be found in the same chapter.

5.15 Summary

A positive tone and atmosphere in your classroom can be created by the use of wall posters, pictures and noticeboards. This can help:

- promote a positive attitude to learning English
- provide extra input for language learning.

These suggestions can be implemented with a minimum of extra resources and effort by getting the students involved in developing their own learning environment. It is also possible to overcome many of the physical problems such as rows of desks and a shortage of duplicating facilities by adopting and adapting the ideas in this chapter. There is no reason why large classes should not be communicative if the resources available are used creatively.

5.16 Consolidation tasks

1 Complete this chart by ticking (√) the options you currently use to present task instructions, supplementary texts etc.

	Blackboard	Handouts	Homemade wall charts	OHP	Notice-board
Instructions					
Texts					
Grammar explanations					
New vocabulary					
Student work					

Are there any ways you can reduce the amount of duplication you need? Are there ways in which you can increase the variety and impact of your presentations?

Decide whether you agree or disagree with the following statements:

a) Using too many handouts can be counterproductive.
b) Learning can be promoted by using more than one medium of presentation.
c) The problem with notebooks is that students always make mistakes in copying.

2 Go back over the chapter and make a list of the resources you might want to acquire to supplement your teaching.

Is the item available locally? If not, what alternative(s) can you think of?

3 Look at the activities on pages 51 and 53. How would you organise your classroom in order to carry out the suggested activities as quickly as possible.

5.17 Further reading

There is a growing selection of books on the use of visual aids in language teaching including Morgan Bowen 1982. Holden 1978 and Wright 1975 are useful introductions. Mugglestone 1980 and Shaw and de Vet 1980 both deal with using the blackboard and Wright 1985 is a useful source of pictures to copy.

6 A way forward

Teaching is a dynamic process and integrating new ideas into our practice is an essential part of professional growth. Introducing communication into the classroom does not mean the rejection of previous practice and material. Areas such as grammar and pronunciation remain important although our approach to these may become more concerned with how the language is used than with the teaching of rules for their own sake. The essence of the communicative approach is a change of emphasis in your methodology. You need to seek out every opportunity to increase involvement and maximise the quality and quantity of the interaction in the classroom. For example, pair and group work can be appropriately used for exam preparation as students get a lot out of joint essay preparation and small group discussion of test items etc. It is really a case of examining everything that we do and asking how we can make it more meaningful and communicative. Such an approach highlights the importance of the teacher being a manager and there are ways in which you can prepare yourself for this new role.

6.1 Developing as a teacher

The most important quality to develop is the capacity for self criticism. This means that you should think of ways of improving your skills. These include:

Self-evaluation
This involves looking at your own performance. Some key areas you might look at are:
- the way you organise the physical seating
- the instructions you give
- the way you set up pair and group work.

Self evaluation is helped by the use of observation sheets which set out examples of positive and negative teaching behaviour. It is possible to construct your own observation sheets. For example, an earlier version of the checklist on instructions on page 30 was constructed by teachers who started by discussing the criteria for good and bad instructions. Other useful activities for self evaluation include making an audio (or video) tape of your own teaching. Analyse the tape critically with the help of questions like:

- Do I ask too many questions?
- Do I answer my own questions without giving students a chance to answer?
- Can the students understand my questions/instructions?
- Is my voice clear?   etc.

Work at improving your weaknesses. You will find lots of advice in the books suggested for further reading.

Peer observation

One of the best ways of improving as a teacher is to get a sympathetic colleague to come and watch you teach, providing feedback on your teaching. This can be done with the help of an observation task e.g.

OBSERVATION TASK

Watch the lesson and discuss the answers with the teacher who has just taught.

The aims
Did the teacher achieve the aims of the lesson?
 Were the aims of the lesson clear?
 Were they appropriate to the class?

The teacher
Did the teacher manage to create a positive relationship with the class?
 Did the teacher establish good eye contact with the students?
 Did the teacher make a conscious effort to pay attention to all the students?
 Was the teacher's voice clear and audible?
 Did the teacher cause any learning problems e.g. by standing in front of the blackboard?
 Was the teacher aware of the problems and difficulties faced by the students?

The students
Were the activities appropriate for the students?
 Did the teacher ask the students questions? Were they able to answer them or not?

Were the students encouraged to ask questions or not?
How did students communicate with the teacher?
Was there any student/student communication?
How did students communicate with each other?
Did the teacher make an effort to prepare students for the activity?
Were the students involved throughout the lesson?

Classroom management
Was the lesson effectively managed?
Did the teacher try to arrange the seating in class to suit the activity?
Were the instructions clear?
Did the teacher use the student's names?
Did the teacher monitor what the students were doing?
Was there a clear start and finish to the lesson?
Were any materials which were needed distributed quickly and effectively?

Use of teaching aids
Were the teaching aids used effectively?
Was the handwriting on the board or OHP legible from all parts of the room?
Was any equipment that was needed ready for immediate use?

On the whole, it is best for an observer to focus on particular aspects of the lesson each time that they watch you teach. It sometimes helps to tell observers what you see as your own weaknesses so that they can help you overcome them. Remember that we are not always the best judges of our own performance, so make sure you are ready to be open to comments and advice.

It is also very useful to watch other teachers at work. You should retain your own style and personality as a teacher and adapt what you see to your own situation, but looking at other teachers is a very good way of acquiring new techniques and ideas.

Develop your own resources
It is very important to start collecting materials and ideas. Interesting pictures from magazines, challenging puzzles, articles etc, are worth collecting even if you do not have immediate use for them. Make sure that

your materials are properly kept and stored, (see Morgan Bowen 1982 and McAlpin 1980).

Collaborate with colleagues
Many teachers have successfully set up formal and informal arrangements for exchanging teaching materials and ideas. Try doing it in your own school. A good starting point is to set up a 'Materials File' with examples of pictures, texts and activities used to supplement the textbook.

Join a national or international teacher's organisation
Many teacher's groups are very active and joining these can be a source of support and professional contact.

Start a programme of self-development
Do you work at improving your knowledge of English and the way that it works? Have you ever been to a conference? Have you ever attended a short course? Do you read any professional journals? If the answer to these questions is 'no' you are missing out on opportunities to improve yourself and, however modestly, you should try to start a programme of self-development.

Although the number of journals, teacher's handbooks and mutual support groups are multiplying it is still up to you to make the effort and we recommend that you set your own targets for self-improvement. For example, after reading this book you might decide to set the following targets for the coming term:

I will try to use English for all my instructions.

I will try to introduce a genuine communication game by the last week of term.

You can then plan your strategy for gradually achieving your targets over a period of time.

Task 1
Think of an area in which you want to improve e.g. setting up your classroom. Make a list of desirable teaching behaviour in this area. Consult a reference source after you have made your own list (see suggestions for further reading). Use the checklist next time you teach and see how many of the items are totally automatic to you. If there are gaps consider ways of improving your performance.

Task 2
Make yourself a target for your next term e.g. 'I will try and introduce pair

and group work'. Try and map out a programme for achieving your target. Set the programme out in the form of a timetable i.e. 'In week 1, I'll . . .'

Commentary
Very few targets can be achieved overnight and planning is an essential part of change. A good programme will map out what you intend to do and when. In practice you may decide to modify your plan but you should always know why you are doing it. If possible, compare your programme with advice given in the relevant sections of this book.

6.2 Developing your methodology

In the earlier chapters we argued the need to plan in the gradual introduction of pair and group work through a process of learner training. We have also tried to provide some ideas for introducing more communicative activities in a traditional context. This process can take weeks or months to achieve but as soon as this is done you can think about developing long-term solutions to one of the biggest problems of large class teaching which is the mixed ability group.

6.3 Mixed ability classes

People do not learn languages at the same rate. This fact, coupled with a move away from streaming according to ability in many countries, means that the majority of teachers in large classes have to cope with not only different levels of linguistic expertise but different levels of intelligence and motivation as well.

Some of the problems teachers frequently mention in relation to mixed ability classes include how to:
- prevent bright students from getting bored or the weak ones from being left behind
- avoid aiming at the average students to the exclusion of the others who also need stimulus and help
- control students who want to disrupt the lesson.

It is important not to forget that these 'problems' probably exist in most classrooms because students are individuals, although the difficulties of catering for different learning styles, interests and needs are more acute and may be more difficult to solve in a large mixed ability class, (see Breen and Candlin 1980 on learner variation).

6.4 Individualisation

Individualisation has for a long time been recommended as the solution to many of the problems of mixed ability classes. In individualised learning students can:

- work at their own pace
- pursue work that is relevant to their own needs and interests
- develop the capacity to work independently of the teacher
- learn in a way that suits them.

Individualisation can help with the problems of mixed ability for the following reasons:

- it provides involvement. It is vital that students are engaged at each stage of the lesson.
- it develops responsibility. Students become responsible for their own learning. They work towards individual goals in which they compete with themselves while co-operating with their classmates.
- it increases motivation. Many students prefer to follow areas which interest them.

We can provide individualisation in a variety of ways. Students can:

- work on different tasks according to their level, needs and interests.
- work at different aspects of the same task.
- work on tasks that can be carried out at a variety of levels.

The ideal environment for individual work is a self access centre, but a great deal of progress towards independent learning can be made even where facilities such as the ones in the illustration have yet to be achieved.

Figure 6.1

Task 3
Look back at Chapters 2 and 3 of this handbook. Which parts of the discussion are particularly relevant to the problems of mixed ability classes?

Commentary
Introducing individualisation is a long-term project. Students need to be trained to work independently of the teacher in a positive environment. They need to get used to a change of teacher role, and the discussion here should be seen as an extension of, rather than a departure from, the suggestions in the earlier sections.

As suggested earlier, responsibility and involvement are key concepts and if you have a mixed ability class you should start by asking yourself whether you have implemented the suggestions in Chapters 1, 2 and 3. In particular you should ask yourself:

- Have I made enough effort to get to know my students? (see page 13)
- Am I doing what I can to get them involved and develop responsibility? (see page 25)
- Have I got them started on the road to independence through pair and group work? (see page 42/45)

If the answer to these questions is 'yes' you can then think about implementing some further solutions to the problems of mixed ability teaching.

6.5   Ideas for mixed ability classes

Have a management policy
When you get to know your students you will soon get an idea of the level of their ability in English. (Try not to be influenced by their performance in other subjects; language learning and academic prowess do not always go together.) As soon as you have a picture of the ability of the class you should aim to manage:

- the questions you ask.
  Allocate easy questions to the less able or confident, and more difficult ones to better students. You should also be careful about the choice of victims or volunteers.
- the composition of working groups.
  You should have a policy regarding the formation of groups. At times it can be very useful to put strong and weak students in the same group. This is particularly true of any task where students have to collaborate to get something done, (e.g. task on page 78). Weaker students may

have something important to contribute which is not directly related to their knowledge of English. The need to help each other develops an important social skill and the stronger students can also get valuable practice by initiating conversation and providing linguistic information to the others. For other tasks, e.g. grammar exercises or writing, it may be better to separate the stronger and weaker students. You should then set different tasks for each group. Students can and should help themselves but there should also be opportunities for extending the able and helping the weak. Giving students different tasks in small groups is an ideal way of doing this, e.g. the same picture composition could be given to all the students in the class, with different tasks for groups at the same level. *Task 1* involves the least processing and production, *Task 5* the most.

Task 1

Arrange the jumbled sentences in order to tell the story in the pictures. (All the sentences are correct). Copy the story in your notebook.

Task 2

Arrange these sentences in order to tell the story in the picture. Some of the sentences are not true. Copy the correct story into your notebook.

Task 3

Write a story with the help of the pictures provided.

Task 4

Write a story with the help of these pictures. Decide on a different heading for each section.

Task 5

Each member of the group has one part of a picture story. Describe your picture to the other students. Agree on the best order and write a story.

Motivate your students

In a mixed ability class you should try to develop ways of motivating all your students. Some students are not motivated by marks or academic success and therefore need to feel that there is a reason for learning English. Pop songs and articles about English-speaking singers, foot-ballers etc., are well tried ways of increasing motivation and interest with adolescents, but one of the greatest motivators of all is success. Students who are confident and able may be motivated to try harder by the occasional failure or low mark, but weaker students can easily decide to abandon all hope if they sense that they are not making any progress in relation to the others in the class, (see Bailey 1979). Make sure you praise weaker students if they make progress (however modest) and encourage them whenever you can. It might work wonders! Weaker students also need a lot of revision and recycling of material. See if this can be made more interesting by introducing some variety e.g. by revising vocabulary in crossword puzzles or using an exercise from another textbook. It has also been observed that low achievers ask fewer questions because they are afraid of looking foolish, so it is very important to check discreetly that these students are following your instructions and explanations. As we said earlier (see page 48) it is a good policy to go to the weaker students as soon as you start a period of pair or group work.

Keep something up your sleeve

In large classes the best students often finish early. It is therefore very useful to have something which will occupy them while others are finishing. Build up a series of tasks which can be given to students who finish early. These can be:

- games and puzzles
- lists of words to learn
- comic strips with the captions missing for students to complete
- pages from other textbooks
- ideas from magazines for EFL teachers
- short texts from magazines and newspapers.

Figure 6.2   From *It's Your Turn* by Donn Byrne, MEP.

Ideally these fillers should be covered with plastic material to protect them. They can be kept in a box and it can become part of the students' normal routine to come quietly to the front and collect something to work on. Remember the Turkish proverb 'Idle men tempt the devil'!

Think through the tasks you give

- *Use open-ended tasks.* In a mixed ability class, tasks which are relatively open-ended often work better than tasks which have only one solution. For example, a task like the LEGO game (page 78) can be completed at different levels of language. This would give the better students a chance to use more complicated structures and vocabulary if they wish.

- *Rethink traditional activities.* Some traditional activities are not really suited for large mixed ability classes because it is very difficult to cater to the different levels, e.g. listening comprehension work with the machine at the front of the class is of limited value if all the students are given the same questions and listen to the tape the same number of times, as the better students will get to the answers first. If possible you should try setting up listening comprehension activities in small groups of similar ability. If you have only one or two tape recorders, the machines can be circulated while the other students are working on other skills. The great advantage is that students get the chance to control the machine and check and recheck their understanding with each other. This is not possible with the full class.

- *Introduce new approaches.* A class library (see next section) or project work (see pages 115 to 120) are ideally suited to the needs of mixed ability classes and you should consider introducing these if you have time.

Introduce a class library

Introduce a class library or reading card scheme if you have not done so already. A properly managed reading scheme can allow for individualisation and communicative language use. For this you need:

- a range of reading material at different levels of difficulty (this can be anything from home-made reading cards to a selection of the readers and reading boxes now available).

Figure 6.3

From *Reading Choices* by David Jolly, CUP.

- a series of workcards to go with the texts.

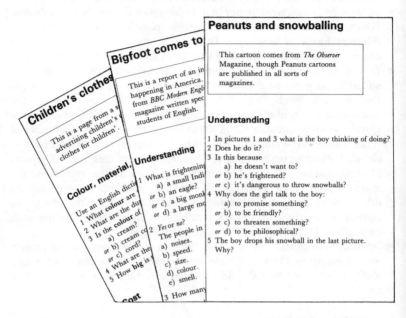

Peanuts and snowballing

This cartoon comes from *The Observer* Magazine, though Peanuts cartoons are published in all sorts of magazines.

Understanding

1 In pictures 1 and 3 what is the boy thinking of doing?
2 Does he do it?
3 Is this because
   a) he doesn't want to?
   or b) he's frightened?
   or c) it's dangerous to throw snowballs?
4 Why does the girl talk to the boy:
   a) to promise something?
   or b) to be friendly?
   or c) to threaten something?
   or d) to be philosophical?
5 The boy drops his snowball in the last picture. Why?

Bigfoot comes to

This is a report of an in happening in America. from *BBC Modern Engli* magazine written spec students of English.

Understanding

1 What is frightenin
   a) a small Indi
   or b) an eagle?
   or c) a big monk
   or d) a large mo
2 *Yes or no?*
   The people in
   a) noises.
   b) speed.
   c) size.
   d) colour.
   e) smell.
3 How many

Children's clothes

This is a page from a s advertising children's clothes for children'.

Colour, material, Understanding

Use an English dicti
1 What **colour** are
2 What are the du
3 Is the **colour** of
   a) cream?
   or b) cream c
   or c) cord?
4 What are the
5 How **big** is

cost

Figure 6.4

- a system for keeping records of the books read.

TITLE	BORROWER	BORROWED	RETURNED
The War of the Worlds	Carlos Silva	6/6	13/6
Gandhi	Maria Santos	13/6	

Figure 6.5

All these would be supplied if you bought a reading box but these are expensive and may not be suited to your needs. You might prefer to make your own. For detailed guidance in setting up reading schemes see Hedge 1985. Setting up your own reading scheme takes time but the advantages are considerable.

Independent reading develops:

- knowledge of the language
- knowledge of language use
- reading skills and strategies
- a positive attitude to reading.

It provides a genuine opportunity for students to work at their own level and pursue their own interests, and once students have been trained to use a reading scheme it affords rewarding moments of peace and quiet.

6.6 The rationale for project work

Project work helps to bridge the gap between language study and language use. As such it is an opportunity to link classroom learning with the world outside. The essential characteristics of a project are:

- students have a task to complete. The options include making something e.g. build you own solar reflector; organising an event e.g. a visit to the UK; gathering information from different sources in order to produce something e.g. a leaflet.

  The project should be comprehensive enough to incorporate a variety of sub-tasks which involve the students in skills such as writing, note-taking, interviewing strangers, reading reference material etc. In this way projects give students integrated practice in all the language skills.
- students have the option of completing the task in a variety of ways. This gives students a chance to pursue an area that interests them. It also allows the members of a mixed ability group to find their own level.

The results of project work can be presented in different ways e.g. a poster, a completed product, a report, a radio programme etc, and students can make full use of their non linguistic skills such as art work or photography within a language learning context.

Projects can take a variety of forms. They can be based on individual work or group work. They can be carried out in the classroom or they can take students into the community. They can be short-term (i.e. completed in one or two lessons) or long-term (i.e. taking a large part of the academic year). They give students the opportunity to pick up a lot of language without it being formally or explicitly taught. When projects involve other people students develop useful social skills and most students gain great satisfaction from completing a major piece of work in English. The confidence and self discipline acquired from doing project work often results in a much more positive attitude to learning English.

Although they are more difficult to manage, group projects are particularly valuable in large classes as students gain satisfaction in that what they do individually or in small groups significantly contributes to a final collective event or product. It is no wonder that the traditional school play, which is a kind of project with a real purpose, i.e. to entertain others, is usually highly successful when it is well organised (see Dougill 1987, Wessels 1987). However, project work requires time, both inside and outside class, and it is by no means an 'easy option'.

6.7 Introducing project work

The introduction of project work needs to be thought through very carefully and the following checklist should be of help.

Preparation
1 Decide on the time available for project work. (It would be wise to start with a small-scale project which can be carried out within the school itself.)
2 Choose a topic. (In theory, students should choose their own topics but this would be unwise with students who do not have experience of such work. You would also need to consider the sources of information you have available. A list of ideas for topics can be found in the next section.)
3 Establish the objectives (you should have some idea of whether the end product is social e.g. an event, linguistic e.g. a report or something the students make. Try not to be too ambitious at the start.)
4 Research the topic area. What will be the sources of information for you and your students? (Add to the list of ideas in the next section.) How will you gain access to them? Where do you need to write for information? When will you inform outsiders and how?
5 Plan in the linguistic support students will need for each stage of the project e.g. Will they need model reports? Will you need to teach them how to ask questions and interview people? Will they need help finding and reading sources?
6 Arrange interviews and outside speakers if possible. (Make sure you keep records in case you want to repeat the project.)
7 Make a timetable for the project. Consider:
When/how you will gain the students' interest.

When/how you will establish the aims and objectives.

When/how the linguistic support will be introduced.

What other support students will need during the project. Think about and plan sessions when you can look at their progress.

When/how students might get training if equipment is needed.

When/how the final presentation of the project is to be arranged.

Execution

1 Present the project to the students. Engage their interest, tell them how much time they have, make sure they know exactly what they have to do and arrange a time for the presentation.

2 If necessary introduce and practise the skills they need.

3 Give students guidance in the form of worksheets and questionnaires. Encourage students to supply their ideas as well.

4 If the task involves going out to meet or interview people then give students confidence by organising a rehearsal. Read through any letters they write etc. All of this helps reduce anxiety.

5 Keep checking on progress.

Feedback

1 Give students time to start preparing for the final presentation.

2 Decide how and when you will correct their language.

3 Decide how and when they will get feedback on how the project will be carried out.

Task

Go through the sample project in the next section with the help of the checklist on introducing project work you have just looked at. Make a note of any additions or modifications you would need to introduce before using a version of this project with your students.

6.8 A sample project

	INFORMATION FOR TOURISTS
Level	Intermediate to advanced
Aim	To produce a set of information for English-speaking tourists to the students' town or region, which can be put on display.
Time	6 to 8 hours of classwork.

Preparation   Collect together input material; think through the
                 stages of the project with the checklist; provide the
                 material needed to support the display.

Procedure

1 Bring in examples of information to tourists and get students to
  look at them. Some of the information may be about the UK,
  others may be locally produced. Devise a worksheet to help
  students look critically at the material and analyse the
  information which is included (or not included), its clarity etc.
  At different stages students could look at the design and layout
  and the language used. Get students to comment on the verb
  forms and adjectives. Students could work in groups and look
  at similar or the same brochures and compare notes as to which
  is best and why, before moving on to the next stage.

2 Explain to students that their objective is to produce some
  information on the town/region for a particular audience (these
  could be real tourists in a local hotel or an imaginary group, but
  it is important to know their age, interests etc). Tell them they
  will present their information in the form of a poster with
  pictures, text, maps etc. Divide them into working groups and
  give them time to decide on areas that are likely to be of
  interest (e.g. castles, restaurants etc). Each member of the
  group, or pairs within the group, should take responsibility for
  looking at a particular area, producing photographs etc. Tell the
  students when they will meet again and give them time to
  collect material (one or two weeks).

3 At this point you may wish to give the class a parallel writing
  activity in which they use a model as the basis for their own
  piece on a local landmark or attraction. Decide whether other
  forms of support are required.

4 Give students time to prepare and edit their work in class.
  Encourage group discussion.

5 Stage an exhibition in which the class get a chance to walk
  round to see other pieces of work. The presence of native
  English speakers would be a major source of motivation, so try
  to invite some even if they are teachers. You might even try to
  persuade the tourist office to let you hold your exhibition there,
  but make sure you tell the students what you hope to do and
  arrange it well in advance.

6 Arrange a time for feedback.

Comments
This is a project with a high degree of control. If a lot of time is available for English there is no reason why it should not be extended to include street interviews.

6.9 Ideas for project work

It is possible to build projects around any topic or field of activity. However, what can be done is dependent on the availability of resources, and the ideas which follow have the overseas situation in mind.

Individual projects
- Planning a holiday, e.g. a trip to an English-speaking country. Activities might include writing for information, planning the trip, going to an airline office, enquiring about visas etc.
- Writing a case study of a famous person.
- Writing a guide to . . . (a place or an activity the student knows well).
- Exploring a subject of interest e.g. space travel, and preparing a dossier.

Group projects
- A class play.
- Planning and setting up an English event (e.g. a tea party). This could involve researching recipes for traditional foods like scones, cooking (at home!), inviting a native speaker to share tea, looking at the history of tea and how it is prepared in England etc.
- Preparing information about the town or region and exchanging this with a group of English-speaking children.
- Writing a case study of an English speaker or an English-speaking community that lives in your country.
- Putting together a class newspaper or radio programme. (The newspaper could be displayed on the wall rather than duplicated).
- Looking into areas of the life of an English-speaking country such as the system of government, the press, homes and gardens, etc.
- A questionnaire survey of visitors to your town.
- Design projects for which students either need to produce something and/or write a report. Some of these may rely entirely on creativity e.g. design a new product. Others may tap their ability to apply scientific principles e.g. research and build a model of a solar reflector.

The success of these depends on materials and informants being available.

The following strategies will help you maximise your resources.

- Brainstorm all sources of authentic English material, e.g. the radio (including the BBC World Service), libraries, The British Council, local firms, English teachers, native speakers of English, multi-national companies etc. Get your students to do the same. Inform anyone you wish to involve in advance. Ask their permission, tell them what to expect and if necessary how to respond to students. Prepare students linguistically and socially for any encounters.
- If you find informants to interview send a small group rather than individuals.
- Build up collections of travel brochures, information sheets etc when you receive them. They might be useful in future.
- Invite people to come to speak to the students. Most people are only too happy to come for the experience, but they need to be aware of linguistic constraints so tell them what the students are likely to understand.
- See if teachers of subjects such as science might be interested in a joint project which is carried out in English. (Sciences and social sciences are particularly appropriate because of the amount of scientific literature which is in English.)

6.10 Feedback

Some teachers and students are concerned about the degree of freedom in tasks like project work and worry about errors and how to correct them. In general, we are a lot more tolerant about errors today than in the past and error is regarded as a natural part of learning (see Norrish 1983 and Revell 1979). However, feedback is a major source of motivation in any form of learning. We like to know what we have done wrong and we generally welcome constructive advice on improving our performance. Feedback on oral performance can be particularly difficult to organise in a large class and students need to be trained to accept that on the spot correction is neither necessary nor desirable.

6.11 Areas for feedback

Feedback on communicative performance should go beyond the correction of grammatical error. In conversation for example areas for feedback may include:

- grammar
- appropriacy of vocabulary and expressions
- fluency and pronunciation
- body language e.g. the way speakers sit may affect our understanding of what they are trying to say.

Feedback is helped by a record of what students do, and video recordings can be extremely useful, but in many places a tape recorder is all we can hope to use in the course of normal teaching.

6.12 Using a tape recorder

Tape recording students allows you to:
- identify areas of weakness which can form the basis of subsequent lessons focussing on accuracy and the presentation of new language.
- conduct discussions which focus on how something should or should not be said.
- keep a record of how students have improved.

A very short extract (say 30 seconds) could form the basis of a subsequent lesson. If you decide to do this you should make sure that it is likely to be of general interest. Make a transcript of what is on the tape so that students can have extra support when they listen to it, as the quality of the recordings is usually quite poor. Do not correct what is on the tape and try and keep hesitations and false starts.

If tape recording is impractical you might sit in on one or two groups and make notes of student performance in areas such as grammar, fluency and pronunciation, appropriacy of vocabulary and expressions. Your notes and/or the taped data could then form the basis for one or more of the following tasks.
- Put up a list of utterances which the students used and ask them to decide on whether they are correct or not.
- Ask students to decide whether or not the expressions they used were appropriate or not.
- Ask students to decide on whether certain forms/pronunciations were correct or not.
- Put up a list of incorrect forms and ask students to correct them.
- Ask students to work out a range of appropriate alternatives for words and expressions used at certain points in their discussion.
- Ask learners to use expressions which were correct, but inappropriate, in a more appropriate context.

Note that the objective is to get students to formulate their own judgements as to what is correct or not. Remember to be constructive and encouraging, and always try to mention things which are good as well as make suggestions for improvement.

A similar procedure can be used with writing, where it is also very useful to get students to compare their own performance to a model.

Once students get used to the idea of reflecting on their own performance it becomes possible to give students the chance to carry out feedback tasks independently of the teacher, (see Nolasco and Arthur 1987).

6.13 Summary and conclusion

The discussion of project work brings together the ideas behind the main theme of this handbook: how to involve all the students in a large class in using English communicatively, both in and out of school.

Teaching communicatively usually involves the introduction of change at some stage. To achieve this in a large class we suggest a gradual approach in which the following occurs:

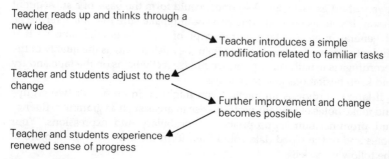

Teacher reads up and thinks through a new idea

Teacher introduces a simple modification related to familiar tasks

Teacher and students adjust to the change

Further improvement and change becomes possible

Teacher and students experience renewed sense of progress

The main ingredients for success are:
- conviction in the aims and objectives of the methods you want to introduce.
- a willingness to take account of student expectations and work towards modifying these if necessary.
- a willingness to mould ideas, activities and materials to suit your particular students and their needs.

In some cases progress may be slow. In others success may be achieved after a short space of time. The important thing is to analyse the reasons for success and failure and to keep trying to do better. Students in large classes have at least as much need for communicative language teaching as those privileged to learn in small groups. It is a challenge, but our experience is that teachers who have met this challenge achieve a heightened level of professional satisfaction through working in a classroom where students gain pride and confidence in being able to use English for communication independently of the teacher.

6.14 Consolidation tasks

1 One solution to the problems of mixed ability is that students should complete the same activity at different levels.
Complete this table. One example has been done for you.

Activity	Weaker students	Middle group	Better students
Dictation	Give students a version of the dictation with a few gaps e.g. 1 in 5	Give students a version of the dictation with 50% missing	Ask students to complete the task without support
Role play in which some students are reporters getting information from a government official			
A storytelling activity in which students tell a traditional story in English (there is a version of 'Little Red Riding Hood' in many countries)			
Activity in which students design a questionnaire to find out about pets of the people in the class			

2 Use the checklist on project preparation (pages 116) to help you write out the procedure for a project you might be able to carry out with your class in the near future.
3 Write down three areas of practice you will change as a result of reading this book.

6.15 Further reading

Teachers wishing to develop their skills might be interested in some of the books in the DES Teacher Education Project *Focus Books* published by Macmillan. They were not designed with foreign language teaching specifically in mind but cover all the subjects in the curriculum. They offer useful guidance in areas such as classroom management and handling classroom groups. There is also a growing collection of teacher's resource books available on the market and you are encouraged to read widely. Fried-Booth 1986 is a source of further ideas on project work.

Bibliography

Bailey, K M, 'An Introspective Analysis of an Individual's Language Learning Experience' in *Research in Second Language Acquisition: Selected papers of the Los Angeles Second Language Research Forum*, S Krashen and R Scarcella eds., Newbury House, 1979

Barnes, D, *From Communication to Curriculum*, Penguin, 1975

Breen, M P and Candlin, C N, 'The Essentials of a Communicative Curriculum in Language Teaching' in *Applied Linguistics*, Vol I, No 2, 1980

Breen, M P, Candlin C N and Waters, A, 'Communicative Materials Design: Some Basic Principles' in *RELC Journal* Vol 10, No 2, 1979

British Council ELTI, *Pair & Group Work in a Language Programme*, British Council, 1980

Brown, G, *Microteaching*, Methuen, 1975

Brumfit, C, *Communicative Methodology in Language Teaching*, Cambridge University Press, 1984

Candlin, C N, *The Communicative Teaching of English*, Longman, 1981

Carrier, M and The Centre for British Teachers Ltd., *Take Five*, Harrap, 1980

CILT, *Syllabus Guidelines*

Delamont, S, *Interaction in the Classroom*, Methuen, 1976

Ellis, G and Sinclair, B, *Training for Learners of English*, Cambridge University Press, 1988

Frank, C and Rinvolucri, M, *Grammar in Action*, Pergamon/Prentice Hall, 1983

Dougill, J, *Drama Activities for Language Learning*, Macmillan, 1987

Fried-Booth, D, *Resource Books for Teachers: Project Work*, Oxford University Press, 1986

Furlong, V, 'Interaction Sets in the Classroom' in *Explorations in Classroom Observation*, Stubbs, M and Delamont, S eds., John Wiley & Sons, 1976

Gower, R and Walters, S, *Teaching Practice Handbook*, Heinemann Educational Books, 1983

Harmer, J, 'What is Communicative?' in *English Language Teaching Journal*, 36/3, 1982

Harmer, J, *The Practice of English Language Teaching*, Longman, 1983

Harrison, A, *A Language Testing Handbook*, Macmillan, 1983

Hedge, T, *Using Readers in Language Teaching*, Macmillan, 1985

Holden, S, (ed) *Visual Aids for Classroom Interaction*, Modern English Publications, 1978

Hughes, G S, *A Handbook of Classroom English*, Oxford University Press, 1981

Kennedy, C and Bolitho, R, *English for Specific Purposes*, Macmillan, 1984

Kerry, T and Sands, M, *Handling Classroom Groups*, Macmillan Education, 1982

Klippel, F, *Keep Talking*, Cambridge University Press, 1984

Littlewood, W, *Communicative Language Teaching – An Introduction*, Cambridge University Press, 1981

Littlewood, W, *Foreign and Second Language Learning*, Cambridge University Press, 1984

Marland, M, *The Craft of the Classroom*, Heinemann Educational Books, 1975

McAlpin, J, *The Magazine Picture Library*, Allen & Unwin/Heinemann, 1980

Morgan Bowen, B, *Look here! Visual Aids in Language Teaching*, Macmillan, 1982

Mugglestone, P, *Planning and Using the Blackboard*, Heinemann, 1980

Naiman, N et al., *The Good Language Learner*, Ontario Institute for Studies in Education

Nolasco, R and Arthur, L, 'Try doing it with a class of forty!' in *English Language Teaching Journal*, 40/2 April, 1986

Nolasco, R, and Arthur, L, *Resource Books for Teachers: Conversation*, Oxford University Press, 1987

Norrish, J, *Language Learners and their Errors*, Macmillan, 1983

Porter Ladousse, G, *Resource Books for Teachers: Role Play*, Oxford University Press, 1987

Revell, J, *Teaching Techniques for Communicative English*, Macmillan, 1979

Richards, J C and Rodgers, T S, *Approaches and Methods in Language Teaching*, Cambridge University Press, 1986

Rixon, S, *How to Use Games in Language Teaching*, Macmillan, 1981

Rixon, S, *Developing Listening Skills*, Macmillan, 1987

Rubin, J, 'What the good language learner can teach us' in *TESOL Quarterly*, 1975

Shaw, P and de Vet, T, *Using Blackboard Drawing*, Heinemann, 1980

Stubbs, M and Delamont, S, *Explorations in Classroom Observation*, John Wiley & Sons, 1976

Vincent, M, *English Teachers' Handbook*, Voluntary Service Overseas, 1978

Vincent, M, Foll, D and Cripwell, K, *Time for English*, Collins, 1985

Wessels, C, *Resource Books for Teachers: Drama*, Oxford University Press, 1987

Widdowson, H, 'The Teaching of English as Communication' in *English Language Teaching Journal*, 27/7, 1972

Williams, E, *Reading in the Language Classroom*, Macmillan, 1984

Willis, J, *Teaching English Through English*, Longman, 1981

Wright, A, Betterridge, D and Buckby, M, *Games for Language Learning*, Cambridge University Press, 1979

Wright, A, *1000 Pictures for Teachers to Copy*, Collins, 1985

Useful sources for classroom activities

Carrier M and The Centre for British Teachers Ltd., *Take Five*, Harrap, 1980

Frank, C and Rinvolucri, M, *Grammar in Action*, Pergamon, 1983

Klippel, F, *Keep Talking*, Cambridge University Press, 1984

Maley, A and Moulding, S, *Poem into Poem*, Cambridge University Press, 1985

Morgan, J and Rinvolucri, M, *Once upon a time*, Cambridge University Press, 1983

Nolasco, R and Arthur, L, *Resource Books for Teachers: Conversation*, Oxford University Press, 1987

Rixon, S, *How to Use Games in Language Teaching*, Macmillan, 1981

Revell, J, *Teaching Techniques for Communicative English*, Macmillan, 1979

Rinvolucri, M, *Grammar Games*, Cambridge University Press, 1984

ELT magazines and journals with practical teaching ideas

Modern English Teacher, Modern English Publications, P.O. Box 129, Oxford OX2 8JU, England

Practical English Teaching, Avenue House, 131–133 Holland Park Avenue, London W11 4UT, England

English Language Teaching Journal, (a journal which aims to combine theory and practice) Oxford University Press, Walton Street, Oxford OX2 6DP, England

English Teaching Forum is distributed by American embassies abroad. Questions about subscriptions should be addressed to the American Embassy in the capital city of the country you are living in.

Contacts and exchanges

In Britain and Ireland

Groups

Class-to-class penfriend schemes, linking a class of yours to a class in Britain are normally arranged through Ministries of Education. Most of the links are organised with France, Germany, Italy, Spain and the Scandinavian countries but some schools may welcome links with other countries. If you have problems you can write directly to:

Links section, Central Bureau for Educational Visits and Exchanges, Seymour Mews House, Seymour Mews, London W1H 9PE

OR

Federation Internationale des Organisations de Correspondances et d'Echanges Scolaires, 29 rue d'Ulm, 75230 Paris, France

Individuals from EEC can write to

Poste Européene de l'Amitié, c/o Maison de l'Europe, 37 rue Francs-Bourgeois, 75004 Paris, France

From outside EEC

International Youth Service, PB 125, SF-20101 Turku, Finland

In America

Groups

World Pen Pals, 1690 Como Avenue, St Paul, Minnesota 55108, USA

Individuals or groups can write to:

International Friendship League Inc., 55 Mount Vernon Street, Beacon Hill, Boston, Mass 02108, USA

In Australia

Individuals and groups

International School Correspondence, UNAA (New South Wales), GPO Box 9820, Sydney, New South Wales 2001, Australia

In New Zealand

Individuals

Five Continents Company Ltd., Bethells Road, Waitakere, Auckland, New Zealand

For contacts in non-English speaking countries students can write individually to: International Youth Service or Poste Europeene de l'Amitie (see above for address) or directly to:

Pädagogischen Austauschdienst, 5300 Bonn, Nassestrasse 8, Postfach 2240, West Germany

OR

The Pen Pal Directory, Pennefosten, PO Box 117, 4700 Nastved, Denmark

OR

Centralnamden for Skolungdomsutbytet, Skolgrand 2, 11724 Stockholm, Sweden

The magazine *Practical English Teaching* also offers a chance for contacts and exchanges with English teachers in Western Europe.